Marketing

Career Guide

Marketing Overview, Scopes and Trends in Marketing, Job Growth and Outlook, Common Types of Marketing Positions, Education, Qualifications, Salary Expectations, Interviews and More!

By Christopher Wright

Foreword

Marketing is integrated in everything we do – whether we like it or not. I'll give you an example; imagine the first few hours of a typical person's day; chances are after waking up in the morning, they'll take a bath, brush their teeth, eat breakfast, drink coffee while watching the morning news, or preparing their kids' lunch for school before heading off to work – that's just for the first few hours! Can you imagine how many goods and services a person on an average day encounters? Possibly around 100 or more! What about the times when you buy 'important things' like furniture, appliances, or products and services that costs thousands of dollars, or something that you use regularly? If you live in a large house, the goods and services you'll encounter is potentially in the tens of thousands. Marketing doesn't stop in the products or services that we consume, but also in the ideas we 'buy' in terms of our health, our overall wellness, and even in choosing our leaders.

Marketing is the art of buying and selling – ideas, products, services etc. and it always involves making a decision; it all depends on your choice as a consumer. What kind of newspaper do you want to read on your way to work: the one that's handy and easy to hold, or the one that'll provide you with more information? Where do you prefer to buy your coffee: is it from the one that serves your favorite cup, or the more established one where every employee goes to?

You see, whether we are aware of it or not, marketing is a huge part of our lives (unless you choose to live in a cave, and just eat organically grown produce for the rest of your life) especially in today's modern world where everything is driven by buyers and sellers. It helps us to make informed choices, and filter out the best options – thanks to the marketing specialists that uses their unique skills and customize marketing strategies in order to meet the consumer's needs related to the various goods and services.

All of the aforementioned are perhaps the reason why you are somewhat in the verge of making a decision to pursue careers related to marketing. You probably recognized that this is both an exciting and challenging field where you could make your mark. However, this profession is rapidly becoming sophisticated and more specialized since the dawn of the Information Age and the rise of social media which is why you need to ensure that you are knowledgeable about this field so that you can learn the various roles and functions of marketing professionals and decide which marketing career suits you best.

Table of Contents

Get Your Marketing Game On!

Buying and selling is the name of the game in the field of marketing therefore it's not quite accurate to say that marketing is solely about selling products or services. If you want to be a successful marketer, you have to know the art of buying and selling because these concepts go hand in hand – and this is one of the most important pointers you'll learn from this guide book. These days, it seems that the word "marketing" is a concept used by almost everyone particularly in the world of social media. From celebrities (how do I create my own personal brand?) to politicians (is the candidate marketable?) to entrepreneurs (how can I market my idea, product, services online/ offline?) to ordinary 'netizens' (how can I attract traffic to my blog? Or how can I be seen?). However, it's quite hard to grasp what marketing really means especially for a newbie looking to start a career in this field, or an undergraduate that's still undecided on what specific marketing job to pursue. In fact, even those who are already in the field still struggle when asked, "What do marketers do?"

If you're reading this career guide, you probably wanted to gain a clear understanding of what marketing is especially from a career standpoint. You're in luck because this book will tackle exactly what you need to know in this profession as well as the key job opportunities available in this field.

Most colleges and business schools including marketing professionals don't really provide guidance on the wide array of career paths in the field of marketing which is why it's best to learn from a marketing professional like me who have been in the game for quite a long time. I will gladly share with you the hard – earned wisdom I learned along the way, and how the information and recommendations I'll share to you have helped me and others to start and sustain a career in this field.

If you're considering becoming a marketing professional, or you're someone who's looking to acquire additional knowledge then this book is for you.

If you don't exactly know "what marketers do," well you're not alone – and because there's no exact or single answer to that. Consider this field as somewhat a playground for people who are good at multi – tasking but still specialized in certain jobs. You'll soon find out that each marketing career path is somehow interconnected with each other, and in order to gain specialization in one marketing profession, you need to combine all the knowledge, skills, methods, strategies etc. you can get along the way from other marketing careers.

If you don't clearly understand the job of marketing professionals, it'll be hard for you to understand what career options are available, and what marketing profession is right for you which is why it's best that before we dive into what kind of degrees you should take, what kind of jobs are available, the traditional vs. digital marketing fields, how to land your first job, etc. we first take a look at what marketing in general is all about.

A career in marketing is simply one of the most sought after and timeless professions in the world with lots of opportunities waiting for you. Time to get your marketing game on!

Chapter One: Marketing Overview

Selling, promoting, or marketing goods, services, ideas, and even personal brands have become increasingly complex especially in today's tech driven world. The job of a marketer became harder than ever before because of the competition online as it created various issues for people in the supply chain. Gone are the days when marketing professionals promote products and services only through direct and traditional forms of advertisements such as those that we see, read, and hear on TV, radio, billboards, newspapers, events etc. Thanks to the internet, selling and promoting became much easier in many ways, and less expensive but perhaps quite specialized and more competitive than ever before.

Can you imagine how a designer sustain his/ her line of clothing when potential customers can purchase the latest fashion or buy a cheaper copy straight from online stores before the fashion designer even had a chance to properly promote them? How do you think movie distributors compete with pirated copies of international movies that can easily be downloaded online long before it was even marketed or released in abroad? How about businesses who already gained a bad reputation for their products through remarks on social media even before they try to sell it to the public?

What I'm trying to say is that indeed, we are a society of consumers but because of the advancement of technology and the domino – effect of social media, marketing campaigns and advertising decisions are becoming extremely challenging for professionals today.

In this chapter, you'll be given an overview about the field of marketing, the definition, main functions/ roles of a marketing professional including the differences between traditional and digital marketing as well as marketing and customer insights.

What is Marketing?

There are various definitions of the term marketing, and even if you read them all, you'll still find it quite difficult to understand because it's usually vague and broad. Part of the problem is that most marketing professionals like to make things seem complicated than they really are for some reason – perhaps job security? The term "marketing" covers a wide array of functions, roles, meanings, and activities just like how we define the word "business." It's broad because it has a wide scope but for me, it can be boiled down by just two words: systematic selling.

Marketing is a systematic approach of selling products, services, ideas, brands etc. to people/ customers/ consumers. It can also be defined as the process of identifying, and designing certain goods and services that people find valuable to satisfy their needs or wants. It also comes from understanding the psychology of the market – the reason why some people buy a certain product or not. Marketing is a system that can help entrepreneurs to identify gaps in the marketplace, recommend or offer new products/ services, suggest to potential customers new ways of solving a problem, and/or influence the consumer's mind to make a certain products or services a necessity even if most of the times it's not.

The American Marketing Association defines marketing as "the process of planning, and executing the conception, pricing, promotion, and distribution of ideas, goods, and services to create exchanges that satisfy individual and organizational objectives."

From all the definitions aforementioned, we can say that the term marketing encompasses a wide range of activities that help marketers effectively sell their goods and services and also help promote their respective companies or organizations. Everyone who is in business needs marketing expertise because without it the business will ultimately fail. Businesses is all about making profit, they will never make any money if they will refuse to market their products or services, and the value of their company; no matter how superior their product is, or how well – structured their organization is. Therefore marketing is tantamount to creating value not just for the businesses' customers but also for their shareholders and society as a whole.

Marketing is the bridge that connects the value of the consumers and what the companies or businesses can offer. Value is the benefit that's received by the consumer whether if it's functional (ex: HD TV), emotional (products that are worn or used for status), societal (leaders that can make a change) etc. It includes the tactics and methods that can help companies and organizations better understand their consumers' needs, perceptions, and preferences. It's a system that helps a company or organization focus on how they can create value and communicate it to their target market in the most efficient and effective way possible.

From a career standpoint, the profession of marketing is all about uncovering the tangible and intangible needs of the consumers, and delivering value to them in the most effective way either to gain profit or achieve a certain goal such as getting a politician in office.

Are You Inclined for Marketing?

Everything is literally marketable – but not everyone is inclined to become a marketer. Like anything else in life, for one to effectively communicate the value, use, or potential of a certain product or service – it will take knowledge, skill set, and attitude. All of these are important if you want to become a competent marketing professional. Companies, organizations, and even you as an individual needs an effective marketing strategy in order to convey what you want or what you truly are especially if you're applying for a marketing position. You need to know how to sell yourself, and develop your own personal brand so that the interviewer or the hiring manager will resonate with you and remember to hire you!

An effective marketer should have the ability to be flexible because creating a marketing campaign for various organizations both online or offline is going to be quite challenging and mind boggling at times especially if you don't know your customers, or the whatever goods or services you're planning to promote/ sell to the public.

The expertise of marketers nowadays is no longer seen as some form of luxury but as a vital part of business strategy. Needless to say, the marketing department can make or break a business in the long run; this is why marketing professionals are highly valued in any company.

Marketers are there from start to profit – it's an essential part of any company looking to launch a new product or service. You are expected to be part of the project from birth, through conceptualization, to promotion and sales, and even after – sales. Marketing professionals especially those that are involved in retail also use their products to help consumers make informed choices.

Even if there are various roles, activities, and functions involved under the umbrella of marketing, marketing professionals usually have the following traits:

- Marketers are always interested in why people buy the things they buy.

- Marketers are fundamentally inclined to the sales value or the "saleability" of a certain item.

- Marketers are usually more interested on how they can create ideas about a particular product or service than the goods itself.

- Marketers are focused on both the short – term and long – term results of their strategies and campaigns.

- Marketers have that certain charm that makes it easier for them to sell almost anything.

Traditional vs. Digital Marketing

There are some marketing roles that can't really be divided into solely traditional marketing or digital marketing because most roles are a combination of technology and traditional components. As I've mentioned in the introduction, some marketing careers are often intertwined, it's just a matter of specialization.

Traditional marketing professions today will mean that the tasks may not be dominated by digital whereas digital marketing careers will mean doing tasks that are focused in using technologies, and various digital marketing strategies. Specialized roles are usually placed on online marketing professions such as social media management, digital marketing management, web community management, search engine management, search engine optimization, etc.

The next chapter will focus on the main components of what marketing professionals do in general whether it's more inclined in the traditional or digital space. You'll also learn the 4 Ps of marketing, the industry trends, and the main scope of the sector so that you'll have knowledge on what this field encompasses.

Chapter Two: Scope, Roles, and Trends of Marketing and Marketing Professions

The answer to the broad question of "What do marketing professionals do?" is these four activities; (1) customer and market insights (2) marketing planning (3) marketing execution (4) marketing optimization. Regardless of the roles or specializations under the umbrella of this field, the four activities aforementioned is what marketing professionals do on a daily basis whether it's for a small marketing project of a business or SMEs, promotions for the launching of a new product or service, marketing campaigns for a particular politician or organization, or simply by creating a personal brand online – marketers integrate these four concepts in every task they take.

The Four Activities of Marketers

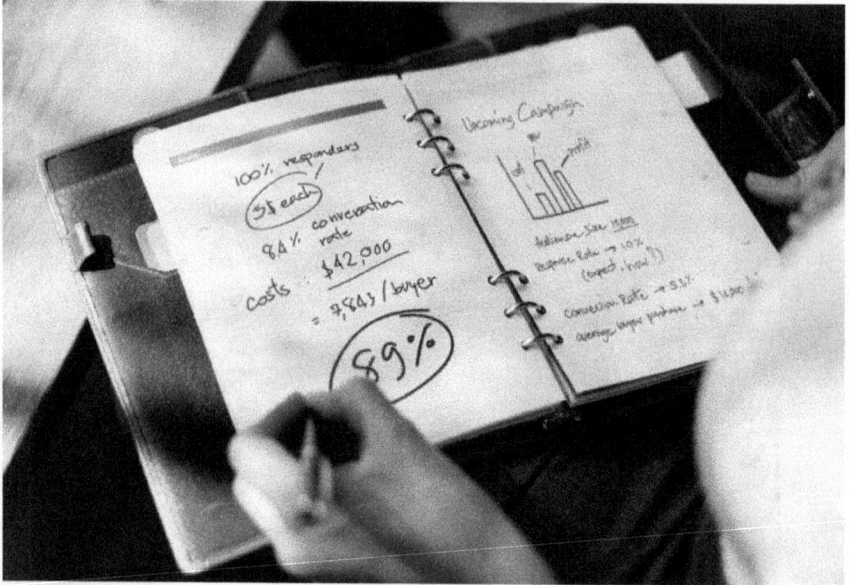

Marketing is all about the sequential planning and implementation of these four concepts, and in this section we will tackle all of these methods so that you'll have a general idea on how you will tackle your future marketing career regardless whether you'll be more on the traditional or on the digital media side.

Customer and Market Insights

Before getting into the nitty gritty details of how a product or service will be promoted, marketing professionals make sure that they know their customers, consumers, or target market through using the method of customer and market insights. This method helps any marketer to predict the projection of a certain product category or industry in order to fill the needs or wants of the consumers in an efficient and effective way. All great marketing campaigns and successful launches is the result of superior customer and market insights. You see, anyone can produce superior products or quality services but if it doesn't connect to the target market, and the public don't see anything that's uniquely valuable, even if the product or service is the crème de la crepe, it will ultimately fail.

Success in marketing highly depends in knowing not just your customers but also your competition and the overall market condition. However, having a great product/ service as well as knowing how you can give more value than your competition is not enough to create success if the market condition is not favorable at the moment. For example, let's say you or the company you're working for created a high – tech gadget like a drone that can carry humans safely and effectively from one location to another, and you found out a way to make it affordable for everyone. However, because the market condition in general is not yet ready for in – flight technologies or "personal aviation" the product has a huge chance of failing simply because of lack of customer/ market insights.

Customer and market insights starts with the intimate understanding of the consumer – including his/ her unspoken wants, needs, fears, expectations and aspirations. Various research methods are used to gain nearly accurate information about people's psychology, preferences, etc. It's definitely a tedious process but keep in mind that world – class products is not possible without world – class marketing insights. As a future marketer, it's a must for you to know your potential customers down at their core. You must always be interested to know their big 'why.'

Here are some of the functions related to market research or market insights:

- Analyzes the purchasing behavior of consumers

- Analyzes response patterns of what makes consumers desire a particular product or service

- Research about establish ways to increase the consumer's desires.

- Find out information on what makes consumers respond to a particular trigger or stimuli

- Organizes marketing information in a way that will benefit others in the supply/ marketing chain.

- Conducts focus group, surveys, test – buys, and incorporates various research methods that could help the team design and execute the right marketing campaigns to sustain or change the buyer's behavior.

- Interested in studying and researching information about the target market with specific goals in mind to provide something useful for advertisers and sales team.
- Customize or structure a research method that would best benefit and bridge the gap of the consumers and the product/ service that a company is planning to offer.

Market Planning

The next thing that marketers do is to apply the information they gained through their market insights and include it in their planning. Marketing planning in general is where marketers identify new products/ services or enhance existing ones to better meet their consumer's need. There are four elements under marketing planning that are used for a successful marketing campaign; this is also known as the 4 Ps of Marketing:

- Product
- Price
- Place
- Promotion

Product

The job of a marketing professional is not just creating what products/ services to produce but also identifying what product/ service could bring something unique and valuable in the existing marketplace. Marketers develop products or enhance an existing one to offer something – either a benefit or feature that's not currently available to the consumers. Marketers in general work side by side with the research team, engineering team, and design/ advertising team to deliver a superior and valuable product/ service.

Price

The marketer may also decide at what price to sell the product or service based on their market insights and research. Price can often times make or break a product. If it's too expensive for the target market, sales volume will suffer but if it's too cheap then it wouldn't be profitable.

Marketers help in finding the price that can maximize sales and profitability.

Place

After the product is perfected, it's the marketers' job to properly deliver it to the end user like deciding the right venue or strategy on how the products can reach the customers or the best method for customer acquisition (ex: direct marketing, third party such as distributors/ retailers/ social media/ internet marketing etc.). All of these decisions will ultimately affect all aspects of the marketing plan and implementation.

Promotion

After deciding the most efficient channel to deliver the product, the next step that most marketers face is creating a plan on how to stimulate or attract consumers. It's every marketers job to be able to create demand through various promotional activities both traditional or digital so that the target customers will be encourage to try out a new product, or show to them that they need it. The goal is to not just sell a product/ service, the main goal is to create repeat customers. Usually, a marketer is limited by the company's marketing budget which is why it all comes down to how creative and strategic a marketer is when it comes to finding the right promotional program that will both maximize profitability and sales within the budget.

The marketer is also in charge of coming up with a strategy in order to achieve the company's/ client's target goals such as annual sales, visions, reputation, business plan etc.

Here are some of the functions related to market planning or advertising:

- In charge of making sure that the target consumer is attracted to a product/ service through tapping into the public's needs.

- Advertisers or those involve in the market planning are highly creative people and has expertise in using multi – sensory tools that will entice or provoke emotional connection or reaction in consumers.

- They're a master when it comes to making people 'buy' the idea of how a product/ service/ brand can change the consumer's lives for the better.

- They are naturally persuasive, creative, and emphatic because all of these traits are essential to not just sell a product/ service to a consumer but also makes them trust the company. Building trust is key in making sure that the business will have repeat customers and clients.

Marketing Execution

The next step after research or insights and planning is of course execution. As the saying goes, "an idea is just an idea without proper execution." The goal of a marketer is to implement the plans and research that went into the process. You'll be in charge of how to motivate, persuade and influence the consumers to buy the product/ service you're promoting. This is also where specialized marketing professionals like advertisers, digital marketing team, consumer promotion, trade marketing, social media management etc. comes in because it's their job to get the message out there and it requires a great deal of marketing expertise and skill. If you're not a specialized marketer, you'll most likely be working with them once you're already at the execution stage. The next page will show you some of the functions related to marketing implementation.

Direct/ Traditional Marketing:

- If done through direct marketing, the marketing professional must be a master in the art of selling because it is usually done through various means such as offering a product/ service through phone sales, copywriting, leaflets, coupons, video blogs, online graphics, brochures etc.

- A marketer must also know how to present solutions and provide answers to customer queries. He/she should also learn how to build trust and connect to the consumers by being 'presentable,' and is likeable to attract customers.

Digital Marketing:

- A digital marketer in general must be tech – savvy in order for him/ her to connect better with consumers in the online marketplace.

- They must have the ability and expertise in attracting customers using various online tools such as blogs, social media pages, emails, apps, banner ads as well as SMS/ MMS ads via mobile phones and other digital distribution channels.

- The digital marketer must be creative to successful implement the marketing plan and should learn to adapt to the fast and changing pace of technology and online world. Content as they say is king in today's media tech – savvy world. It's important that one should be able to execute plans in a timely, cost – effective, relevant and personal manner.

- Even traditional marketers must become proficient in using digital marketing technologies and find a way to integrate the traditional and digital to potentially reach a wider spectrum of consumers.

Events Marketing:

- Events such as concerts, exhibits, openings, seminars, conferences, contests etc. are where marketers sell or promote products.

- Event marketers usually create a specific program for the sole purpose of selling or promoting a product/ service as this can create an enticing environment for the potential consumers. This is also where free samples are given in order to create a positive image for the product/ brand/ service.

- Event marketers are also connected with various outlets for sponsorship purposes. Being tied up to a credible organization or brand can definitely benefit the product/ service being promoted, this is all part of marketing strategy and execution.

Marketing Optimization

Some marketers are tasked to measure, analyze, and continually improve the performance and efficiency of the existing marketing campaigns. Optimizing a brand, product, or service is crucial because it will help drive maximum effectiveness of the marketing campaign and investment. This is sort of the after – sales assessment that marketers use to further improve their products/ services.

Here are some of the functions related to marketing optimization:

Sales Promotion:

- Also known as relationship marketers, people in sales should have the ability to make sure that the customers they've attracted will keep coming back for more through using various sale promotions such as loyalty cards, sampling, trade shows and events, merchandising, packages etc.

Public Relations:

- Establishes and promotes favorable relationships not just to the target consumers but also to the general public, to businesses, organizations, and media as part of trust building.

- PR specialists are the after – sales marketers and they must be experts in using the power of words to build, sustain, and continuously influence people when it comes to promoting a certain brand, product/ service, or organization.

- Must know how to troubleshoot and provide damage control in case of unforeseen circumstances to maintain consumer/ public trust as well as the credibility of brands/ business/ products/ services.

- Must be excellent in both written and spoken language as it involves creating speeches, and press releases.

Chapter Three: Marketing Job Growth and Outlook

The U.S. Bureau of Labor Statistics estimates that the employment of marketing professions is expected to grow through the next few years at the time of this writing. The fields of digital marketing will most likely be in demand as consumers are getting more and more comfortable with making purchases online through e – commerce, websites, and social media. Jobs in the traditional marketing fields or other forms of traditional advertising could decline or become limited because consumer behavior is quickly changing due to the explosion of tech and online savvy economy. This is why traditional marketers and advertisers will have no choice but to adapt and combine strategies that would encompass both traditional and digital media since more and more consumers are purchasing and being influenced online. Those who can navigate around the online world and can maximize the communication tools that are available will get more job opportunities in this field in the next decade.

In this chapter we will get into some stats regarding the job growth in the marketing field, the type of organization you can work for, the future career path for marketing professionals, the top cities and companies in the United States in need of marketers as well as the overall outlook so that you'll have an idea what kind of opportunities awaits a prospective candidate like you.

Marketing Job Growth Statistics

According to Monster.com, in 2012, there were around 200,000 jobs related to marketing that are available in the U.S., and they also estimated that by the year 2022 it will increase by around 24,000 more. According to the statistics of projected job growth obtained by the U.S. Bureau of Labor Statistics (BLS), they forecasted that from 2014 to 2024, positions for marketing managers will have higher than average projected job growth in the country. At the time of this writing, marketing managers is the top 13 among the best paying occupations in America.

In addition, the U.S. Bureau of Labor Statistics Public also found out that the Public Relations positions are predicted to grow about the same as the average of all jobs. Unfortunately, promotions managers, graphic designers as well as traditional advertisers are now a bit below the average since most businesses and corporations are looking to hire more digitally savvy marketers for today's fast changing world.

These statistics are very important especially for you as a prospective marketing professional because you need to understand how marketing occupations will shift in the next few years so that you can acquire the skills, knowledge, and expertise that businesses will need in the future. If you know the marketing careers that will be in demand in the near future then you can better position yourself, choose the best compensation package, and also take advantage of the opportunities that will arise due to this demand in the industry.

Businesses and companies are planning to spend huge amounts on digital marketers since online is where the marketplace is headed. They are now spending less on traditional marketing professionals, channels and distributors such as print/ radio/ TV advertising as well as events and direct campaigns because the marketing budget will shift to the digital space therefore it's wise to gain technical or digital skills if you want to easily get a marketing job in the next few years.

Here are some other factors to consider:

The Gender Gap

According to Payscale, about 80% of marketing coordinators are women but only 38% of women are at the top such as Chief Marketing Officers and PR heads. This is a significant gender gap and it could be due to generational differences but this clearly reflects that women who wanted to pursue higher positions related to marketing is still quite challenging.

In – Demand Marketing Jobs by City

When it comes to finding a marketing job, it's the same as real estate – it's about location, location, location! Forbes recently ranked the cities in the United States that have a huge demand for marketing professionals. If you are the aggressive type or you're open to working in a super competitive environment then the best place to go to is none other than the financial and business capital - New York City. The Big Apple has two times the number of marketing positions being offered than the next top city which is San Francisco in California though if you are more into startups and you're digitally inclined then perhaps you'll find lots of options here than in New York. Check out the cities that offers various positions for marketing professionals:

- New York City (around 4,000 positions available)
- San Francisco California (around 2,000 positions available)
- Chicago Illinois (around 1,500 positions available)
- Seattle Washington (around 1,000 positions available)
- Los Angeles California (around 1,000 positions available)
- Atlanta Georgia (around 1,000 positions available)
- Washington D.C. (around 1,000 positions available)
- Boston Massachusetts (around 900 positions available)
- Austin Texas (around 800 positions available)
- Dallas Texas (around 650 positions available)

In – Demand Marketing Jobs by Companies

Forbes also ranks the top companies and multinational corporations that are looking to hire various marketing professionals. According to these companies, marketing isn't just essential to attract traffic and acquire customers but also to attract the best workers since marketing also takes care of the company's brand, value, credibility and image. Check out the list of these companies below:

- Amazon.com (E – commerce/ Retail)
- Wells Fargo (Financial institution)
- GAP Inc. (Retail and Fashion)
- Microsoft (Tech company)
- Wyndham Worldwide
- Comcast (Media company)
- JPMorgan Chase (Financial institution)
- Oracle (Tech company)
- Facebook (Tech company)
- Uber (Transportation company)

Type of Organizations You Can Work For

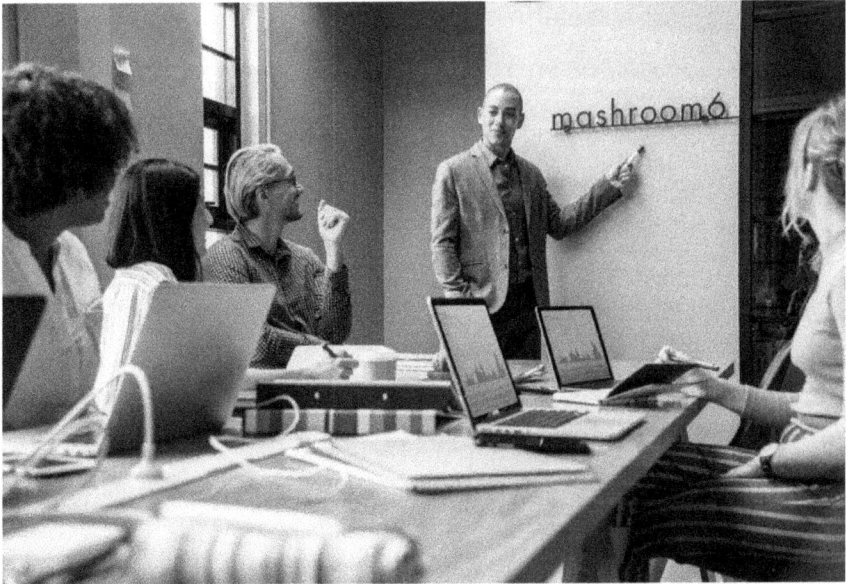

The type of organization you will work for in pursuing your marketing profession will definitely have a huge impact to the direction of your career. Below are the advantages and disadvantages of the four types of organizations that you can apply to:

Agency

Advantages:

- You'll have opportunities to work in various companies including SMEs.

- Marketing jobs especially those that are related in public relations usually require an agency experience.
- You'll be surrounded with experts in various marketing fields that you can learn from.
- Offers good salaries though compensation packages may not always be that attractive

Disadvantages:

- What the client says goes
- Long hours are usually required of you to meet client deadlines
- Marketers are often expected to be on – call depending on the client's requests.
- Marketers are usually faced with lots of competitions for promotions
- The ability to acquire new marketing skills could be limited due to lots of competition or if you'll be assigned to a more specialized task.
- Marketers are at risk of burn out.
- Job security highly depends on business development.

Consulting Firms

Advantages:

- You'll have opportunities to work in various companies.
- Marketers can have the opportunity to transfer into other marketing teams which in turn could gain you technical/ business skills unless the firm is marketing specific.
- Great compensation.

Disadvantages:

- What the client says goes
- Long hours are usually required of you to meet client deadlines
- There will be times of an up or out culture
- Marketers are at risk of burn out.
- You may have to frequently travel and meet clients
- Job security highly depends on business development.

In – House

Advantages:

- Marketers in this kind of organization are usually regarded as the 'experts' and go – to people when it comes to marketing concerns
- You'll have more opportunity to take on leadership roles related to marketing, promotion or sales.
- You can gain lots of skills, knowledge, and experience
- You'll get to have mentors
- Job security is better than other types of organizations

Disadvantages:

- There aren't many employees who can cover up for your position
- Getting top leadership roles could be hard because there's a hierarchy or corporate ladder to work through.
- Marketers may not get as much experience compared to working in consulting firms or agencies that are more directly working with clients.
- Marketers will need to be able to prove the return of investment to bosses and colleagues.

Startup

Advantages:

- Marketers in this kind of organization are usually regarded as the and go – to people when it comes to marketing concerns
- You'll have more opportunity to take on leadership roles related to marketing, promotion or sales.
- You can gain lots of skills, knowledge, and experience since startups are a more hands – on type of organizations
- You'll have the chance to create marketing strategies and handle it from start to profit.
- You'll have the opportunity to be a part of an exciting and innovative working environment.
- You can be part of the pioneer team and a great culture

Disadvantages:

- Job growth will highly depend on how the startup can scale on a fast pace
- Job security is not guaranteed
- There aren't many employees who can cover up for your position

Chapter Four: Qualifications for Aspiring Marketers

Marketing degrees teach students how to promote goods and services to potential consumers as well as analyze the consumer's demands. The marketing lessons you'll learn in school or other marketing courses in general will definitely equip you to work in various areas and in various industries. Marketing degrees and courses provide flexibility because it can be applied to a wide array of business – related work or professions which is the reason why it's very popular and perhaps a timeless career path. Thanks to the wide application of marketing education, these degrees can be studied at a bachelor's level, master's level, and doctorate levels. Each level are tailored for certain goals so that students can be prepared for any types of marketing professions which can range from marketing consultants to college professor.

Marketing degrees also offer opportunities for specialization; some degrees can provide you with a general knowledge that can be applied to almost any type of marketing and business – related careers while some are geared towards a more specialized skill that can be applied in careers relating to quantitative, research, or behavioral marketing. Various specialized marketing degrees especially those that are found at the master's and doctorate levels will also equip students for management roles such as Marketing Director, Brand Manager, and even leadership roles like Chief Marketing Officer and Vice President of Sales.

In this chapter you'll learn the various types of marketing degrees and courses as well as the steps on how you can pursue a marketing career so that an aspiring marketer like you can be qualified and well – educated.

Steps to Qualify for a Marketing Degree and Career

Here's what you can expect from the educational and professional journey in the field of marketing:

Step #1: Complete High School

Almost all marketing professions will require an aspirant to finish a bachelor's degree, and some will even recommend a graduate degree that's either related to business or specialized in marketing. No matter what degree you acquire, obviously you'll never get to college without graduating high school. The subjects you'll learn in high school may not seem to be related to the subject of marketing but if you do well in general subjects like Math, basic Accounting, and English it'll be an advantage for you in pursuing a marketing profession because these subjects will provide you with a solid foundation for various courses particularly marketing and business.

In addition, joining business clubs, student government, or PR - related organizations in your school will also give you a glimpse of the basic tasks you'll eventually do when you pursue a marketing degree in college since these clubs will give you opportunities to promote, sell, and communicate your ideas to fellow classmates.

High school is also the time to discover the specific marketing path you may want to take so that choosing a marketing course in college will be easier for you. If you are more inclined in PR then perhaps it is better if you take up communications; if you like to take on leadership roles then a degree in business management might be best for you etc. You don't really need to identify everything at the onset but it'll be helpful when it comes to deciding what particular business/ marketing course you're going to pursue if you know the subjects you're more inclined with or the field in marketing you could be interested in.

Step #2: Acquire a Bachelor's Degree

Acquiring a bachelor's degree is the standard qualification for any marketing and business – related careers. A marketing degree takes about 4 years to complete, and it's a staple course that's being offered by most universities and colleges nationwide. Marketing courses are usually integrated with a Business Administration degree, and can be taken up as a major with a minor in other marketing – related subjects.

Step #3: Complete an Internship

Before you graduate in college, you'll be required to take up an internship or an On – The – Job training. This is a very important endeavor because it will provide aspiring marketers like you with real – world and valuable hands – on working experience. It will ultimately help students in reaching their prospective employers and also establish professional connections. This is also an opportunity for you to apply the knowledge and skills you've learned in school, not to mention the chance to network and leave a great impression to your bosses so that they can help put in a good word for you or recommend you by the time you apply for a job.

Being an intern is a great and fulfilling experience for many college students as it gives them a glimpse of the kind of career they will take in the near future. Internships may be taken during summer or even after graduation.

Step #4: Gain Working Experience

As what they always say, "you have to start somewhere." Once you've acquired a bachelor's degree and completed your internship, it's time to roll up your sleeves and step into the world of employment. Gaining a working experience even if it's just an entry – level job is something that any internship experience can't match.

If you want to also continue your studies by getting a graduate degree like MBAs or PhDs, or if you plan in applying for a higher marketing positions then gaining a working experience will be crucial. Entry – level marketing careers include the following:

- Marketing Analyst
- Marketing Associate
- Marketing Assistant
- Marketing Specialist

The jobs of these entry – level positions usually involve administrative tasks, market research, and sales work which can definitely be an addition to your qualifications while also providing you with a valuable experience in the field of marketing.

Step #5: Get a Graduate Degree (if necessary)

Depending on your overall career ambition, a graduate degree could provide you with more knowledge, and specialized skills which in turn could lead you to more career opportunities. A graduate degree can also give you an edge if you want to take on management and leadership positions in the future.

Graduate degrees such as Master of Business Administration (MBA) and PhD are usually necessary if you want to climb the corporate ladder or perhaps become a faculty in the academe. There are also other graduate marketing programs that provide a more specialized curriculum like in the field of digital marketing, advertising etc.

Marketing Degree Levels and Curriculum

Depending on the specific marketing career you want to pursue, here's a breakdown of what you can expect from each marketing degree level. An aspiring marketer can obtain not just bachelor and graduate degrees but also certifications from colleges/ universities and even through education programs online.

Certification Program in Marketing

An aspiring marketer can obtain marketing certificates that are usually offered in both undergraduate and graduate programs. Certificate programs are usually intended to provide a tailored curriculum, and it only lasts for a few months and no more than a year. The credits of the certification you acquired could be applied towards a bachelor's / graduate degree or it can also provide additional qualifications when applying for a job. If you want to apply as a college professor in business or marketing related courses, you can obtain a certification in marketing as an added qualification to the degree you're holding.

When it comes to the curriculum, it's usually based on the student's preferences and also on the subjects that are being covered in the certification program. Here are some of the common programs included:

Advanced Marketing Strategies

This is a subject where you'll learn the advanced methods and techniques when it comes to identifying various consumer trends, and it will also teach you on how you can help companies take advantage of these trends.

Skills You Can Gain:

- Ability to identify the needs and wants of consumers
- Gain knowledge on how consumers think and recognize trends
- Ability to recognize marketing strategies that can be helpful to specific business needs.

Management in Marketing

Students will learn how to create effective strategic decisions in order to execute marketing plans that are profitable for the client or business.

Skills You Can Gain:

- You'll be familiar with market – oriented strategic planning
- You'll gain knowledge on how to implement digital marketing and social media marketing

- You'll learn how to design and execute sales promotions

Multi – Cultural Marketing

This program teaches aspirants on how to effectively market to consumers from different nations and cultures.

Skills You Can Gain:

- You'll gain cultural knowledge based on historical data and also market research
- You'll learn to recognize the relation of consumer's needs/ wants to their culture and why or how they buy certain goods or services.
- You'll have knowledge on how to create targeted marketing plans that are customized for buyers from specific cultural demographic.

Associate Degree in Marketing

An associate degree in marketing is best for people who want to gain knowledge about marketing but can't commit to a full bachelor's program. It's also best for people who want start working while acquiring marketing knowledge. An associate degree will allow high school graduates to start working in the field after they've completed 2 years of high school. If the student eventually decides to get a bachelor's degree, the credits you've earned in your associate degree will surely be counted.

When it comes to the curriculum, it's usually based on the student's preferences and also on the subjects that are being covered in the Associate Degree program. Here are some of the common programs included:

Introduction to Marketing

This is where you'll learn fundamental concepts and principles of marketing and business in general.

Skills You Can Gain:

- You'll learn marketing research methods and become familiar with terms related to marketing.
- You'll learn marketing strategies that can be applied to attain business goals.
- You'll understand the basics of consumer behavior.

Principles of Retailing

This subject will provide an introduction to the overall business practices of the retail and sales industry in general.

Skills You Can Gain:

- You'll learn various retail management methods.
- You'll understand how multi – channel retailing and distribution works.
- You'll learn how to acquire, maintain, and also improve relationships with both suppliers and customers.

Buyer Behavior

This subject will teach you the principles of the consumers' buying behavior including the psychological, cultural, emotional, financial factors etc. that affects the habits of consumers.

Skills You Can Gain:

- Ability to take advantage of the consumers' buying trends and patterns which can improve sales
- You'll learn how buyer characteristics can influence purchases of customers.
- You'll become familiar with the connection between profits and buyer habits.

Bachelor's Degree in Marketing

The Bachelor's Degree is the standard degree that an aspirant needs to attain in order to start a career in marketing. It generally provides a comprehensive education regarding business and marketing principles. Students need to graduate with a (4 year) Bachelor's degree so that they will be qualified for entry – level jobs or management positions in companies or multinational corporations.

Aside from the general education and elective courses included, students can expect the following subjects/ curriculum to be included especially when they major a degree in marketing. Here are some of the common courses in the program:

Professional Selling

This is the course where students will primarily be taught on how to sell anything in the most effective and efficient way.

Skills You Can Gain:

- You'll learn how to execute various selling strategies to specific consumers or target market.
- You'll learn how to create a good relationship with potential and existing customers/ clients.
- You'll learn on how you can close a sale.

Introduction to Economics

This course will teach you the fundamental principles and theories behind macroeconomics and microeconomics, and will generally teach you about how the economy operates.

Skills You Can Gain:

- You'll learn how about the law of supply and demand.
- You'll gain knowledge about the connection between tax rates, GDP growth, and unemployment as well as other related concepts that affect an economy.
- You'll learn how to measure the overall well – being and status of the economy.

Statistics in Business

This course will give students an overview of the different methods used in statistics and how it can be applied in business particularly in market research.

Skills You Can Gain:

- You'll learn how to apply the inferential and descriptive statistics to certain business/ market issues.
- You'll understand market probability and distributions
- You'll understand how to use hypothesis testing, market correlation, and also regression.

<u>Master's Degree in Marketing</u>

Marketing degrees usually accomplishes two things: (1) gaining general marketing and management skills, (2) provides a path that's geared towards a more specialized marketing skill or towards an MBA and PhD.

There are various kinds of master's degree available for an aspirant marketer such as Master of Business Administration (MBA) which is the common type, and also Master of Science (MS) in Marketing. Obtaining either degree can definitely provide professional advancement though an MBA is more preferred by companies especially for positions related to management. Master's degree usually takes around 2 years or more to accomplish.

Most master's degree subjects allow significant curriculum tailoring in order to meet the needs of each student. Some of the courses to expect in a master's degree level include the following:

Brand Management

Students who take up this course will learn different branding strategies ranging from brand creations to executions in order to effectively promote a certain product/ service.

Skills You Can Gain:

- You'll learn how to assess the value and also the effectiveness of a particular brand.
- You'll gain knowledge on how to create a new brand and also improve an existing brand.
- You'll become familiar with common branding decisions that brand managers faced in the field.

International Marketing

Students who take up this course will learn how to analyze the consumption and buying behavior of international markets.

Skills You Can Gain:

- You'll understand the difference between the consumers in the U.S. and in abroad.
- You'll learn how to handle various cultural and ethical issues that marketers faced in abroad.
- You'll learn how to identify the main issues that are essential to successfully marketing a product/ service/ brand abroad.

Big Data

This is a course where aspiring marketers learn about the fundamental theories and principles of big data research. You'll generally be taught on how to execute strategies and make use of the big data you've gathered through market research in order to better improve an existing product as well as reach out to more people in a target market.

Skills You Can Gain:

- You'll understand the different technologies and methodologies used to achieve a successful market research.
- You'll learn how to analyze information based from the big data gathered.
- You'll learn how to create prediction models so that you can anticipate the market trend as well as consumer behavior.

Doctorate Degree in Marketing

The Doctorate degree or Doctor of Philosophy is the highest form of educational training that any student can attain. You can only get the prestigious doctorate degree if you successfully pass a Master's degree, and usually the students allowed to take this program are the ones who get an above average grade in their MBAs or Master's degree (depending on the university).

This is an education taken mostly by marketers who are already in management and leadership roles or those who are aspiring to climb the top of the corporate ladder although some companies don't necessarily require it. However, if you plan on becoming a college professor or you want to focus on marketing research, getting a doctorate degree is ideal as it can make you more credible. PhD programs usually takes about 2 to 4 years of completion but it could take longer depending on when a student can accomplish the dissertation or thesis.

Some of the courses to expect in a doctorate degree level include the following:

Quantitative Marketing

This is a course where students will be provided with an overview of the various quantitative methods that are used in marketing and how to conduct their own quantitative research.

Skills You Can Gain:

- You'll become familiar with the various theories of quantitative research.
- You'll learn how to create and conduct original quantitative marketing research.
- You'll have an ability to create a study that can answer certain marketing questions related to the product/ service you will want to know about.

Consumer Behavior Research

This will give you an overview of the past and present research regarding consumer behavior of particular marketing campaigns, products, services etc.

Skills You Can Gain:

- You'll learn about the various consumer behavioral theories.
- You'll gain insight about the consumer's buying psychology, emotions, and goals.
- You'll learn the different techniques and methods that marketers use when conducting consumer behavior research.

Decision Making Behavior

This course will enable you to focus on the psychology behind how consumers make choices in general.

Skills You Can Gain:

- You'll get to apply the mental concepts in order to understand consumer behavior better.

- You'll get to know the underlying reasons of why consumers buy certain products/ services.
- You'll learn how to identify the different psychological principles and how you can apply it within a judgment context.

Chapter Five: Executive and Managerial Marketing Positions

Marketing professions have changed dramatically in the last few decades; new branches of marketing have emerged alongside the development of technologies and communication tools. This is the reason why the career path for an aspiring marketer is not as straightforward and simple as it once was. In the next few chapters we will discuss with you in full detail the top 50 marketing jobs today as well as what you can expect in terms of the prerequisites, tasks, workload, skills needed, career progressions and compensation. We've arranged it in such a way that'll be easier for any newbie like you who's about to embark on this career path.

In this chapter, we'll focus first on the top 10 marketing positions that are in the leadership and managerial levels. You'll get to see the highest marketing positions you can aim in the corporate ladder as well as the qualifications and skills you'll need in order to attain this level. This is advantageous for aspiring marketers like you who's just starting out because it can give you an idea on the kind of knowledge and skills you should pick up along the way while you're still climbing the corporate ladder so that someday you'll be fully equip and competent enough to conquer these leadership roles.

Top 10 Job Profiles

Top 1: Chief Marketing Officer (CMO)

The Chief Marketing Officer is primarily responsible for creating, managing, and overseeing the implementation of a company's overall marketing plan and vision. The job of the CMO is to lay out the marketing plan and objectives that will provide direction for the sales team and marketing departments within the company. He/ she must also know how to communicate the company's vision and mission to various media outlets and customers through the use of different marketing channels.

In general a CMO must possess skills in leadership, and must be exceptional in sales, marketing, communication, data analysis, customer research, and even public relations. Having an experience in the field of sales/ branding/ PR/ traditional or digital marketing for quite a long period of time is definitely an advantage.

The Chief Marketing Officer is the highest position in the marketing corporate ladder and it's usually in the executive level along with the Chief Executive Officer (CEO), Chief Operating Officer (COO), and Chief Financial Officer (CFO).

Estimated Annual Salary: $80,000 to $250,000

Average Annual Salary in the U.S: $187,000

Number of Years and Experience (in the U.S.):

- Less than 1% of CMOs have 1 year working experience
- Around 5% of CMOs have 1 to 4 years working experience
- Around 8% of CMOs have 5 to 9 years working experience

- Around 39% of CMOs have 10 to 19 years working experience
- Around 47% of CMOs have 20+ years working experience

Top Skills Needed:

- Strategic Marketing
- Business Development
- Branding
- Marketing Management

Potential Career Advancement: Chief Executive Officer

Educational Qualifications: Advanced degree in marketing or business – related field plus marketing certifications.

Travel Requirements: Expect extensive travel

Work Schedule: Expect long hours of work

Top 2: Vice President of Marketing

VP of Marketing is usually alongside executive levels such as CMOs. The job of the VP of Marketing is to primarily outline and handle the marketing strategies of the company around the products and services it is offering. Their tasks usually involve branding, advertising, pricing and also creating discount offers.

The VP of Marketing works hand in hand with the research team and is also responsible for evaluating the effectiveness of the existing marketing campaign of the company. He/ she is also in charge with generating ideas for future product development as well as proving the return of investment of the marketing strategies being implemented to other executives and directors. The VP of Marketing is usually where marketing employees in a division directly report and also sits on the executive board of the company.

Estimated Annual Salary: $81,000 to $194,000

Average Annual Salary in the U.S: $155,000

Number of Years and Experience (in the U.S.):

- 0% of VP of Marketing have less than 1 year working experience
- Around 3% of VP of Marketing have 1 to 4 years working experience
- Around 12% of VP of Marketing have 5 to 9 years working experience
- Around 49% of VP of Marketing have 10 to 19 years working experience
- Around 36% of VP of Marketing have 20 + years working experience

Top Skills Needed:

- Strategic Marketing
- Advertising
- Marketing Communications
- Marketing Management
- Product Marketing

Potential Career Advancement: Chief Executive Officer, President, Vice President of Sales and Marketing, Executive Vice President of Marketing, Senior Vice President of Marketing

Educational Qualifications: Advanced degree in marketing or any business – related field are recommended.

Travel Requirements: Expect extensive travel

Work Schedule: Expect long hours of work

Top 3: Marketing Director

The job of marketing directors is to direct and manage marketing strategies. They directly oversee the marketing employees within a department, and are also responsible in specifying the scope of the department's marketing needs. The main duties include the following:

- Creating projects for marketing campaigns
- Creating budgets and concepts
- Helps in resolving team issues
- Maintains in close contact with the clients, suppliers, or executives of the company
- Brainstorm ideas for future product developments
- Measure the progress and results of marketing campaigns
- Collects and analyzes data in order to improve future marketing performance of the company.

Estimated Annual Salary: $41,000 to $145,000

Average Annual Salary in the U.S: $81,000

Number of Years and Experience (in the U.S.):

- Around 1% of Marketing Directors have less than 1 year working experience
- Around 17% of Marketing Directors have 1 to 4 years working experience
- Around 26% of Marketing Directors have 5 to 9 years working experience
- Around 40% of Marketing Directors have 10 to 19 years working experience
- Around 16% of Marketing Directors have 20 + years working experience

Top Skills Needed:

- Branding
- Advertising
- Marketing Communications
- Marketing Management
- Strategic Marketing

Potential Career Advancement: Vice President of Marketing, Marketing Communications Director, Senior Marketing Director, Sales and Marketing Director, Business Development Director

Educational Qualifications: Bachelor's degree in Marketing or any related business – related field; marketing certifications is a plus.

Travel Requirements: Travel may not be required

Work Schedule: Expect slightly long hours of work

Top 4: Global Marketing Manager

The Global Marketing Manager is responsible for overseeing the company's marketing campaigns and budget on an international scale. In addition, he/ she lays out and implements marketing plans for the company in a global level. It is also his/ her duty to establish and maintain relationships with international partners. A global marketing manager also works with various departments to expand the business in a global scale.

Estimated Annual Salary: $60,000 to $145,000

Average Annual Salary in the U.S: $103,000

Number of Years and Experience (in the U.S.):

- Around 1% of Global Marketing Managers have less than 1 year working experience
- Around 14% of Global Marketing Managers have 1 to 4 years working experience
- Around 37% of Global Marketing Managers have 5 to 9 years working experience
- Around 33% of Global Marketing Managers have 10 to 19 years working experience
- Around 15% of Global Marketing Managers have 20 + years working experience

Top Skills Needed:

- Marketing Management
- Strategic Marketing
- Marketing Communications
- Product Marketing
- Project Management

Potential Career Advancement: Vice President of Marketing, Marketing Director

Educational Qualifications: Bachelor's degree in Marketing or a degree that's related to the company's focus area; an MBA may be required.

Travel Requirements: Expect to travel overseas from time to time.

Work Schedule: Expect medium to long hours of work

Top 5: Marketing Manager

A marketing manager is responsible in supervising the sales and marketing team and he/ she is also in charge of spearheading the advertising and merchandising campaigns of the company. Marketing managers can be assigned to overseeing a brand, a line of products, a single product or even the entire company. They primarily combine all the inputs that they've gathered from the creative, advertising, and sales department. They must be well - organized because small changes can create a huge impact in the marketing campaigns and brand of a product or the company itself. They need to know how to properly coordinate with various marketing teams and must be able to meet tight deadlines.

Estimated Annual Salary: $40,000 to $96,000

Average Annual Salary in the U.S: $62,000

Number of Years and Experience (in the U.S.):

- Around 2% of Marketing Managers have less than 1 year working experience
- Around 32% of Marketing Managers have 1 to 4 years working experience
- Around 36% of Marketing Managers have 5 to 9 years working experience
- Around 24% of Marketing Managers have 10 to 19 years working experience
- Around 7% of Marketing Managers have 20 + years working experience

Top Skills Needed:

- Marketing Management
- Strategic Marketing
- Marketing Communications
- Social Media Marketing
- Project Management

Potential Career Advancement: Marketing Director, Senior Marketing Director, Marketing Communications Manager, VP of Marketing, Business Development Manager

Educational Qualifications: Bachelor's degree in Marketing with Master's or Doctorate degree is preferred.

Travel Requirements: Travel may not be required

Work Schedule: Follows an average work week but may require long hours whenever a new marketing campaign will be launched.

Top 6: Marketing Coordinator

The tasks of marketing coordinators usually involve the following:

- Helps in developing and coordinating marketing projects
- Presents campaigns that are in the form of traditional and digital marketing

- Must work with other employees that are outside the core marketing department such as graphic designers, digital marketers, customer service representative, external suppliers, logistics etc.

- Must have strong research skills specifically about consumer trends, behaviors, and buying patterns.

- Public speaking and graphic design skills are an advantage

- Marketing coordinators are available for entry – level positions as well as experienced marketing positions.

Estimated Annual Salary: $31,000 to $54,000

Average Annual Salary in the U.S: $40,000

Number of Years and Experience (in the U.S.):

- Around 6% of Marketing Coordinators have less than 1 year working experience
- Around 66% of Marketing Coordinators have 1 to 4 years working experience
- Around 19% of Marketing Coordinators have 5 to 9 years working experience
- Around 8% of Marketing Coordinators have 10 to 19 years working experience
- Around 2% of Marketing Coordinators have 20 + years working experience

Top Skills Needed:

- Marketing Communications
- Social Media Marketing
- Event Planning
- Email Marketing
- Microsoft Office

Potential Career Advancement: Marketing Manager, Marketing Specialist, Marketing Project Manager, Marketing Communications Manager, Marketing Director

Educational Qualifications: Bachelor's degree in Marketing or major in communications is preferred.

Travel Requirements: Travel may be necessary

Work Schedule: Follows an average work week but may require slightly long hours whenever a new marketing campaign will be launched.

Top 7: Marketing Assistant

The tasks of marketing assistant usually involve the following:

- A marketing assistant usually works within the company's marketing department.

- A marketing assistant is responsible in helping collect and analyze data provided by market researchers.

- The assistant will most likely help in accomplishing various administrative tasks within the marketing department.

- This position is an entry – level job and is the first step for aspiring marketers to start their career in a particularly industry.

Estimated Annual Salary: $27,000 to $47,000

Average Annual Salary in the U.S: $34,000

Number of Years and Experience (in the U.S.):

- Around 15% of Marketing Assistants have less than 1 year working experience
- Around 68% of Marketing Assistants have 1 to 4 years working experience
- Around 11% of Marketing Assistants have 5 to 9 years working experience
- Around 5% of Marketing Assistants have 10 to 19 years working experience
- Around 1% of Marketing Assistants have 20 + years working experience

Top Skills Needed:

- Marketing Communications
- Social Media Marketing
- Knowledge in Microsoft Office Applications such as Word and Excel.

Potential Career Advancement: Marketing Manager, Executive Assistant, Marketing Director, Marketing Specialist, Marketing Coordinator

Educational Qualifications: Associate's degree is accepted but Bachelor's degree in Marketing is preferred.

Travel Requirements: Travel is not required unless you'll be required by the marketing head during business trips

Work Schedule: Regular business hours

Top 8: Product Marketing Manager

The tasks of a product marketing manager usually involve the following:

- Must be highly familiar with the products and brand that a company is offering because he/ she is responsible for constructing a marketing strategy on how to sell it to the consumer to generate the potential maximum revenue.

- He/ she is in charge overseeing how a certain product or brand is advertised, and in charge of how media press releases is seen by the consumers.

- They are usually assigned to work on local, regional, national and even global level.

- They are usually experts in specific products from a particular industry (ex: cosmetics, beverages, household materials etc.)

Estimated Annual Salary: $54,000 to $122,000

Average Annual Salary in the U.S: $89,000

Number of Years and Experience (in the U.S.):

- Around 2% of Product Marketing Managers have less than 1 year working experience
- Around 32% of Product Marketing Managers have 1 to 4 years working experience
- Around 34% of Product Marketing Managers have 5 to 9 years working experience
- Around 25% of Product Marketing Managers have 10 to 19 years working experience

- Around 7% of Product Marketing Managers have 20 + years working experience

Top Skills Needed:

- Product Marketing
- Marketing Management
- Marketing Research
- Strategic Marketing
- Marketing Communications

Potential Career Advancement: Marketing Director, Senior Marketing Manager, Product Marketing Director, Senior Product Manager, Senior Product Marketing Manager

Educational Qualifications: Bachelor's degree in Marketing is required with relevant working experience.

Travel Requirements: Travel may not be required but possible from time to time

Work Schedule: Regular business hours

Top 9: Channel Marketing Manager

The tasks of channel marketing manager usually involve the following:

- Channel marketing managers handle transactions of large companies whenever they decide to sell their products through various channels in the form of retailers, distributors, and other affiliates. Companies do these to reach a wider range of market locally or overseas.

- Works with various entities/ corporations in order to support the sales of the company's products

- Ensures that the distribution outlets will maintain the marketing and branding of the products.

Estimated Annual Salary: $53,000 to $116,000

Average Annual Salary in the U.S: $86,000

Number of Years and Experience (in the U.S.):

- Around 1% of Channel Marketing Managers have less than 1 year working experience

- Around 20% of Channel Marketing Managers have 1 to 4 years working experience
- Around 37% of Channel Marketing Managers have 5 to 9 years working experience
- Around 32% of Channel Marketing Managers have 10 to 19 years working experience
- Around 10% of Channel Marketing Managers have 20 + years working experience

Top Skills Needed:

- Market Research
- Internet Marketing
- Marketing Management
- Strategic Marketing
- Marketing Communications

Potential Career Advancement: Marketing Director, Senior Marketing Manager

Educational Qualifications: Bachelor's degree in Marketing is required with experience in logistics and distribution

Travel Requirements: Expect frequent travel

Work Schedule: Regular business hours

Top 10: Marketing Consultant

The tasks of channel marketing manager usually involve the following:

- Marketing consultants are responsible to advice the marketing department and executives on how to further a certain brand, sales and also helps in providing ways on how to acquire more customers for the company.

- He/ she can suggest ideas in various marketing activities such as content marketing, social media strategy, advertising, branding and design, implementation etc.

- Marketing consultants is someone who's highly connected with various departments and also has contacts to third parties, distribution companies, and relevant suppliers.

- Oversees different marketing campaigns and helps in developing new projects.

Estimated Annual Salary: $33,000 to $101,000

Average Annual Salary in the U.S: $62,000

Number of Years and Experience (in the U.S.):

- Around 5% of Marketing Consultants have less than 1 year working experience
- Around 37% of Marketing Consultants have 1 to 4 years working experience
- Around 24% of Marketing Consultants have 5 to 9 years working experience
- Around 22% of Marketing Consultants have 10 to 19 years working experience
- Around 11% of Marketing Consultants have 20 + years working experience

Top Skills Needed:

- Market Research
- Branding
- Advertising
- Internet Marketing
- Marketing Management
- Strategic Marketing
- Marketing Communications

Potential Career Advancement: Marketing Manager, Senior Marketing Manager, Marketing Director, Marketing Communications Manager, VP of Marketing

Educational Qualifications: Bachelor's degree in marketing, communications, or any business – related field is preferred with other specialized marketing certifications.

Travel Requirements: Travel is not required

Work Schedule: Regular business hours

Chapter Six: Branding and Field Marketing – Related Positions

This chapter will tackle the top 11 to 20 marketing jobs that are more or less related specifically in branding, customer acquisition, and field – related marketing positions. Strong leadership and communication skills are very important with these kinds of jobs because they are primarily in charge of inspiring and supervising the marketing teams that they'll be working with. It's also important they are well – organized and knowledgeable in specific fields of marketing such as database management, customer acquisition, and content creation because this is usually tied up to one another.

Job Profiles (Top 11 to 20)

Top 11: Field Marketing Manager

The tasks of Field Marketing Managers usually involve the following:

- Their primary duty is managing the smooth operations of franchise businesses.

- They are in charge of analyzing the business plans of the franchises, how to scale them, and if these franchises are properly operating in the marketplace.

- They also develop field marketing plans and also handle event marketing for brand/ product promotions.

Estimated Annual Salary: $50,000 to $98,000

Average Annual Salary in the U.S: $67,000

Number of Years and Experience (in the U.S.):

- Around 1% of Field Marketing Managers have less than 1 year working experience

- Around 38% of Field Marketing Managers have 1 to 4 years working experience
- Around 36% of Field Marketing Managers have 5 to 9 years working experience
- Around 19% of Field Marketing Managers have 10 to 19 years working experience
- Around 2% of Field Marketing Managers have 20 + years working experience

Top Skills Needed:

- Market Research
- Event Management
- Marketing Management
- Strategic Marketing
- Marketing Communications

Potential Career Advancement: Marketing Manager, Marketing Director

Educational Qualifications: Bachelor's degree in marketing, communications, business administration, advertising, or any related field is preferred with strong background in sales and retail.

Travel Requirements: Occasional travel may be required especially during events or trade shows

Work Schedule: Regular business hours with occasional long hours to meet deadlines

Top 12: Brand Manager

The tasks of Brand Managers usually involve the following:

- They are in charge of managing how a certain brand is perceived and exposed by the target market.

- They usually work with the staff in various marketing departments.

- The brand managers' job is to analyze the target market, and then design marketing strategies in order to better position a certain product/ service in front of the target consumers. They are also in charge of improving the existing brand/ branding position of a product/ service.

Estimated Annual Salary: $41,000 to $114,000

Average Annual Salary in the U.S: $75,000

Number of Years and Experience (in the U.S.):

- Around 2% of Brand Managers have less than 1 year working experience
- Around 33% of Brand Managers have 1 to 4 years working experience
- Around 37% of Brand Managers have 5 to 9 years working experience
- Around 22% of Brand Managers have 10 to 19 years working experience
- Around 6% of Brand Managers have 20 + years working experience

Top Skills Needed:

- Branding
- Product Marketing
- Marketing Management
- Strategic Marketing
- Marketing Communications

Potential Career Advancement: Brand Marketing Manager, Senior Brand Manager, Marketing Director, VP of Marketing, Product Marketing Manager

Educational Qualifications: Bachelor's degree in marketing, communications, and advertising is preferred.

Travel Requirements: Travel is not required

Work Schedule: Regular business hours

Top 13: Marketing Research Analyst

The tasks of Marketing Research Analysts usually involve the following:

- A marketing research analysts' job is to interpret and understand information based from the market research that the company conducted. They are also tasked to make recommendations based on the date gathered.

- They usually work with the marketing team in order to create and execute a better marketing strategy, maintain the existing customers, and also maximize the potential of a certain product/ service in line with what they've found out from the research.

- They should be knowledgeable about market trends and apply it to improve the consumers' experience.

Estimated Annual Salary: $35,000 to $71,000

Average Annual Salary in the U.S: $49,000

Number of Years and Experience (in the U.S.):

- Around 13% of Marketing Research Analysts have less than 1 year working experience
- Around 63% of Marketing Research Analysts have 1 to 4 years working experience
- Around 16% of Marketing Research Analysts have 5 to 9 years working experience
- Around 6% of Marketing Research Analysts have 10 to 19 years working experience
- Around 2% of Marketing Research Analysts have 20 + years working experience

Top Skills Needed:

- Data Analysis
- Marketing Research

- Proficient in Microsoft Excel
- Proficient in SPSS
- Proficient in SAS

Potential Career Advancement: Project Director of Marketing Research, Marketing Manager, Senior Marketing Research Analyst, Market Research Manager

Educational Qualifications: Bachelor's degree in marketing or any business – related field is preferred

Travel Requirements: Travel is not required

Work Schedule: Regular business hours

Top 14: Demand Generation Director

The tasks of Demand Generation Directors usually involve the following:

- They primary duty is to develop and lead the business' content strategies, customer acquisition tactics, and digital influence in order to produce leads that can potentially acquire more customers or reach a wider audience.

- They are in charge of managing the offline and online marketing campaigns.

- They test demand campaigns as well as automate and implement it.

- They usually work with the sales department.

- They are knowledgeable about B2B or Business to Business marketing and they also nurture potential lead sources.

Estimated Annual Salary: $84,000 to $159,000

Average Annual Salary in the U.S: $130,000

Number of Years and Experience (in the U.S.):

- 0% of Demand Generation Directors have less than 1 year working experience
- Around 13% of Demand Generation Directors have 1 to 4 years working experience
- Around 26% of Demand Generation Directors have 5 to 9 years working experience

- Around 47% of Demand Generation Directors have 10 to 19 years working experience
- Around 14% of Demand Generation Directors have 20 + years working experience

Top Skills Needed:

- Internet Marketing
- Lead Generation
- Strategic Marketing

Potential Career Advancement: Head of Digital Marketing Department/ Division

Educational Qualifications: Bachelor's degree in marketing or any business – related field is preferred. Experience in digital marketing is a plus.

Travel Requirements: Travel is not required

Work Schedule: Regular business hours

Top 15: Demand Generation Manager

The tasks of Demand Generation Managers usually involve the following:

- Their job is to entice more customers to certain product/ services that are being offered through content, and various digital marketing strategies.
- They are in charge of creating an effective ads, and content materials that appeal to their target market.
- They usually work with marketing field agents as well as advertisers on a daily basis.
- Database management and knowledge in B2B is also helpful in accomplishing their tasks.

Estimated Annual Salary: $51,000 to $109,000

Average Annual Salary in the U.S: $81,000

Number of Years and Experience (in the U.S.):

- Around 3% of Demand Generation Managers have less than 1 year working experience
- Around 41% of Demand Generation Managers have 1 to 4 years working experience

- Around 36% of Demand Generation Managers have 5 to 9 years working experience
- Around 20% of Demand Generation Managers have 10 to 19 years working experience
- Around 1% of Demand Generation Managers have 20 + years working experience

Top Skills Needed:

- Internet Marketing
- Lead Generation
- Email Marketing
- Strategic Marketing

Potential Career Advancement: Demand Generation Director

Educational Qualifications: Bachelor's degree in marketing or any business – related field is preferred. Experience in digital marketing is a plus.

Travel Requirements: Travel is not required

Work Schedule: Regular business hours

Top 16: Demand Generation Specialist

The tasks of Demand Generation Specialists usually involve the following:

- They usually work with various marketing teams to ensure that the lead generation aims are met.

- They are in charge of designing, testing, evaluating, automating, and implementing new demand campaigns as well as maintaining the software and database being used.

- They are also in charge of measuring the results of the lead generation plans that's being implemented.

Estimated Annual Salary: $35,000 to $80,000

Average Annual Salary in the U.S: $55,000

Number of Years and Experience (in the U.S.):

- Around 4% of Demand Generation Specialists have less than 1 year working experience
- Around 65% of Demand Generation Specialists have 1 to 4 years working experience

- Around 18% of Demand Generation Specialists have 5 to 9 years working experience
- Around 8% of Demand Generation Specialists have 10 to 19 years working experience
- Around 5% of Demand Generation Specialists have 20 + years working experience

Top Skills Needed:

- Internet Marketing
- Email Marketing

Potential Career Advancement: Demand Generation Director, Demand Generation Manager

Educational Qualifications: Bachelor's degree in marketing or any business – related field is preferred. Experience in digital marketing may be required.

Travel Requirements: Travel is not required

Work Schedule: Regular business hours

Top 17: Email Marketing Manager

The tasks of Email Marketing Managers usually involve the following:

- They are in charge of supervising the marketing teams that are in charge of creating and implementing marketing campaigns across different online channels.

- The teams that they handle are in charge of continuously searching for potential customers so that they can bolster the advertising plans for their products.

- An Email Marketing Manager should also be updated with the latest market trends and must have leadership/ communication skills.

Estimated Annual Salary: $41,000 to $87,000

Average Annual Salary in the U.S: $63,000

Number of Years and Experience (in the U.S.):

- Around 2% of Email Marketing Managers have less than 1 year working experience

- Around 40% of Email Marketing Managers have 1 to 4 years working experience
- Around 47% of Email Marketing Managers have 5 to 9 years working experience
- Around 10% of Email Marketing Managers have 10 to 19 years working experience
- Around 1% of Email Marketing Managers have 20 + years working experience

Top Skills Needed:

- Internet Marketing
- Email Marketing
- Direct Marketing
- Proficiency in HTML
- Customer Relationship Management

Potential Career Advancement: Demand Generation Director, Demand Generation Manager, Demand Generation Specialist

Educational Qualifications: Bachelor's degree in marketing, any business – related field, or an MBA is preferred. Experience in digital marketing may be required.

Travel Requirements: Travel is not required

Work Schedule: Regular business hours

Top 18: Content Marketing Director

The tasks of Content Marketing Directors usually involve the following:

- Their primary duty is to work with content managers and strategists in order to drive more customer demand and create more effective content strategy.

- They lead and also help formulate new content marketing plans to ensure that goals are met.

Estimated Annual Salary: $54,000 to $145,000

Average Annual Salary in the U.S: $92,000

Number of Years and Experience (in the U.S.):

- Around 1% of Content Marketing Directors have less than 1 year working experience
- Around 19% of Content Marketing Directors have 1 to 4 years working experience

- Around 30% of Content Marketing Directors have 5 to 9 years working experience
- Around 38% of Content Marketing Directors have 10 to 19 years working experience
- Around 12% of Content Marketing Directors have 20 + years working experience

Top Skills Needed:

- Internet Marketing
- Social Media Marketing
- Content Management
- Copywriting
- Editing
- People Management

Potential Career Advancement: Demand Generation Director, Demand Generation Manager, Demand Generation Specialist

Educational Qualifications: Bachelor's degree in marketing, any business – related field. Experience in digital marketing may be required. Acquiring marketing certifications is a plus.

Travel Requirements: Travel is not required

Work Schedule: Regular business hours

Top 19: Content Strategist

The tasks of Content Strategists usually involve the following:

- Their main job is to create and develop a content marketing plan.

- They often work with social media strategists as well as other marketing teams in order to deliver a cohesive message to the target market.

- Strong communication skill is a must.

Estimated Annual Salary: $39,000 to $99,000

Average Annual Salary in the U.S: $61,000

Number of Years and Experience (in the U.S.):

- Around 2% of Content Strategists have less than 1 year working experience
- Around 50% of Content Strategists have 1 to 4 years working experience
- Around 29% of Content Strategists have 5 to 9 years working experience

- Around 16% of Content Strategists have 10 to 19 years working experience
- Around 3% of Content Strategists have 20 + years working experience

Top Skills Needed:

- Internet Marketing
- Content Management
- Copywriting
- Editing
- Project Management

Potential Career Advancement: Demand Generation Director, Demand Generation Manager, Demand Generation Specialist, Content Marketing Director, Email Marketing Manager, Content Manager

Educational Qualifications: Bachelor's degree in marketing, communications, any business – related field. Experience in digital marketing is required. Strong background in HTML programming and layout is preferred.

Travel Requirements: Travel is not required

Work Schedule: Regular business hours; flexible time for freelancers

Top 20: Content Manager

The tasks of Content Managers usually involve the following:

- They are in charge with overseeing the creative staff and also help in maintain the marketing materials used for a certain campaign.

- They are in charge of editing the written material and make the tone and style more appropriate for the consumers.

- They review and contribute in the content, graphics, and layout presentation of online tools such as websites, podcasts, videos etc.

Estimated Annual Salary: $35,000 to $84,000

Average Annual Salary in the U.S: $54,000

Number of Years and Experience (in the U.S.):

- Around 3% of Content Managers have less than 1 year working experience
- Around 49% of Content Managers have 1 to 4 years working experience

- Around 27% of Content Managers have 5 to 9 years working experience
- Around 17% of Content Managers have 10 to 19 years working experience
- Around 4% of Content Managers have 20 + years working experience

Top Skills Needed:

- Web Content Management
- Content Management
- Editing
- Project Management
- Marketing Communications

Potential Career Advancement: Demand Generation Director, Demand Generation Manager, Demand Generation Specialist, Content Marketing Director

Educational Qualifications: Bachelor's degree in marketing, communications, any business – related field. Experience in digital marketing is required. Strong background in HTML programming and layout is preferred.

Travel Requirements: Travel is not required

Work Schedule: Expect irregular working hours

Chapter Seven: Top E – Commerce and Social Media Marketing - Related Positions

This chapter will focus on the primary duties and responsibilities of digital marketers particularly in the fields of social media and e – commerce. Digital technologies are rapidly dominating the marketing and sales industry thanks to the internet. The market trend has now shifted to the online world which is why businesses and brands are also adapting these changes in technology by building online presence and creating digital marketing plans to reach their customers online. Digital marketing requires specialized marketing skills but it provides more growth opportunities especially for tech – savvy people who are willing to rise to its challenges.

The jobs listed below will surely be in – demand in the next few decades as worldwide markets and industries continue to adapt to these technological changes. We will discuss more about the world of digital marketing in the next few chapters, for now check out the career paths related to digital marketing and see if this is the kind of profession you want to pursue.

Social Media Director

The tasks of Social Media Directors usually involve the following:

- Their primary duty is to build brand loyalty and create awareness in various social media outlets/ channels.

- They are also in charge of customer service strategy in order to increase their market influence online.

- They usually work with brand managers, sales team, customer service, content managers and other digital marketing teams.

Estimated Annual Salary: $30,000 to $121,000

Average Annual Salary in the U.S: $57,000

Number of Years and Experience (in the U.S.):

- Around 2% of Social Media Directors have less than 1 year working experience
- Around 43% of Social Media Directors have 1 to 4 years working experience
- Around 37% of Social Media Directors have 5 to 9 years working experience
- Around 16% of Social Media Directors have 10 to 19 years working experience
- Around 2% of Social Media Directors have 20 + years working experience

Top Skills Needed:

- Social Media Marketing
- Social Media Optimization
- Media/ Public Relations

- Marketing Communications
- Strategic Marketing

Potential Career Advancement: Demand Generation Director, Demand Generation Manager, Content Marketing Director, Content Manager, Head of Digital Marketing Team

Educational Qualifications: Bachelor's degree in marketing, communications, any business – related field. Experience in digital marketing is required. Experience in social media marketing is preferred.

Work Schedule: Regular business hours but expect irregular hours for any social media accounts update

Social Media Marketing Manager

The tasks of Social Media Marketing Managers usually involve the following:

- They are in charge of the company/ brand's online presence across social media channels.

- They analyze social media trends, create/ engage in social content, and also build brand awareness.

They also need to maintain the blog/ content posts and get ideas from their content team.

- The Social Media Marketing Manager is also responsible in creating a customer service system so that the queries, complaints, and other customer issues will be properly handled.

Estimated Annual Salary: $31,000 to $77,000

Average Annual Salary in the U.S: $45,000

Number of Years and Experience (in the U.S.):

- Around 4% of Social Media Marketing Managers have less than 1 year working experience
- Around 63% of Social Media Marketing Managers have 1 to 4 years working experience
- Around 27% of Social Media Marketing Managers have 5 to 9 years working experience
- Around 5% of Social Media Marketing Managers have 10 to 19 years working experience
- Around 1% of Social Media Marketing Managers have 20 + years working experience

Top Skills Needed:

- Social Media Marketing
- Social Media Optimization
- Media/ Public Relations
- Marketing Communications
- Internet Marketing
- Copywriting

Potential Career Advancement: Demand Generation Director, Demand Generation Manager, Content Marketing Director, Content Manager, Head of Digital Marketing Team, Social Media Director

Educational Qualifications: Bachelor's degree in marketing, communications, any business – related field. Experience in digital marketing is required. Experience in social media marketing is preferred.

Work Schedule: Regular business hours but expect irregular hours for any social media accounts update

Social Media Manager

The tasks of Social Media Managers usually involve the following:

- Their primary duty is to manage the social media page/ accounts, website/s and also the brand's profile and create a good media presence online.

- They are in charge of creating social media campaigns through various means such as videos, infographics, social media posts etc.

- They also supervise and approve creative content from their staff and implement new digital marketing tactics that could attract more traffic to their online channels.

- Multitasking and communication skills are required to handle the daily tasks of managing social accounts.

Estimated Annual Salary: $31,000 to $72,000

Average Annual Salary in the U.S: $44,000

Number of Years and Experience (in the U.S.):

- Around 3% of Social Media Managers have less than 1 year working experience

- Around 67% of Social Media Managers have 1 to 4 years working experience
- Around 25% of Social Media Managers have 5 to 9 years working experience
- Around 5% of Social Media Managers have 10 to 19 years working experience
- Around 0% of Social Media Managers have 20 + years working experience

Top Skills Needed:

- Social Media Marketing
- Social Media Optimization
- Blogging
- Marketing Communications
- Content Management

Potential Career Advancement: Marketing Director, Digital Strategist

Educational Qualifications: Bachelor's degree in marketing, communications, any business – related field. Experience in digital marketing is preferred.

Work Schedule: Regular business hours but expect irregular hours for any social media accounts update

Online Community Manager

The tasks of Online Community Managers usually involve the following:

- They focus on interacting to online customers through various social media platforms and also engage conversations with the target market in forums and various social media groups.

- They are skilled in mediation and online marketing because they know how to relay information of new products, promos, contests etc. to the various communities and groups online.

Estimated Annual Salary: $32,000 to $73,000

Average Annual Salary in the U.S: $48,000

Number of Years and Experience (in the U.S.):

- Around 4% of Online Community Manager have less than 1 year working experience

- Around 69% of Online Community Manager have 1 to 4 years working experience
- Around 20% of Online Community Manager have 5 to 9 years working experience
- Around 6% of Online Community Manager have 10 to 19 years working experience
- Around 1% of Social Media Managers have 20 + years working experience

Top Skills Needed:

- Social Media Marketing
- Social Media Optimization
- Customer Service
- Marketing Communications
- Web Content Management

Potential Career Advancement: Social Media Director, Social Media Manager, Digital Marketing Manager

Educational Qualifications: Bachelor's degree in marketing, communications, any business – related field. Experience in social media marketing is preferred.

Work Schedule: Regular business hours or shifting schedule but expect irregular hours for any social media accounts update.

Social Media Coordinator

The tasks of Social Media Coordinators usually involve the following:

- Their primary duty is to communicate the brand to various social media accounts by generating copies of ads and blogs such as newsletters, event announcements, infographics, vlogs etc.

- They are very good at multitasking as they handle various social media campaigns, social media teams, and also work under strict deadlines.

- They are always updated with the latest internet marketing trends and tools. They also help develop marketing plans using promotional tools online.

Estimated Annual Salary: $29,000 to $50,000

Average Annual Salary in the U.S: $36,000

Number of Years and Experience (in the U.S.):

- Around 8% of Social Media Coordinators have less than 1 year working experience
- Around 80% of Social Media Coordinators have 1 to 4 years working experience
- Around 11% of Social Media Coordinators have 5 to 9 years working experience
- Around 2% of Social Media Coordinators have 10 to 19 years working experience
- 0% of Social Media Coordinators have 20 + years working experience

Top Skills Needed:

- Social Media Marketing
- Social Media Optimization
- Media/ Public Relations
- Marketing Communications
- Web Content Management

Potential Career Advancement: Social Media Director, Social Media Manager, Digital Marketing Manager

Educational Qualifications: Bachelor's degree in marketing, communications, any business – related field. Experience in social media marketing may be preferred.

Work Schedule: Regular business hours but expect irregular hours for any social media accounts update especially if an event or promotional duties is required to be covered.

Digital Marketing Manager

The tasks of Digital Marketing Managers usually involve the following:

- Their primary duty is to create marketing projects using various digital channels and online tools.
- They are in charge of creating an efficient and effective advertising tactic in the digital world to market their company's products/ services.
- They are focused on brand loyalty, and they are experts when it comes to e – commerce, SEO, and can adapt to the ever – changing digital space.

Estimated Annual Salary: $40,000 to $96,000

Average Annual Salary in the U.S: $64,000

Number of Years and Experience (in the U.S.):

- Around 1% of Digital Marketing Managers have less than 1 year working experience
- Around 39% of Digital Marketing Managers have 1 to 4 years working experience
- Around 39% of Digital Marketing Managers have 5 to 9 years working experience
- Around 18% of Digital Marketing Managers have 10 to 19 years working experience
- Around 2% of Digital Marketing Managers have 20 + years working experience

Top Skills Needed:

- Social Media Marketing
- Social Media Optimization
- Email Marketing
- Search Engine Optimization
- Content Management

Potential Career Advancement: Marketing Director, Head of Digital Team

Educational Qualifications: Bachelor's degree in marketing, communications, any business – related field. MBA in marketing and working experience in e – commerce is preferred.

Work Schedule: Regular business hours

Digital Strategists

The tasks of Digital Strategists usually involve the following:

- They are the ones who determine how to properly position the digital services/ products online.

- They must be experts in analyzing large quantities of data and be able to identify the keys to a successful digital campaign.

- They must also be knowledgeable in how to outsmart the competitor's line of products or services and be able to apply the date they've gathered to better understand the current market trends.

Estimated Annual Salary: $38,000 to $100,000

Average Annual Salary in the U.S: $61,000

Number of Years and Experience (in the U.S.):

- Around 3% of Digital Strategists have less than 1 year working experience
- Around 48% of Digital Strategists have 1 to 4 years working experience
- Around 33% of Digital Strategists have 5 to 9 years working experience
- Around 14% of Digital Strategists have 10 to 19 years working experience
- Around 2% of Digital Strategists have 20 + years working experience

Top Skills Needed:

- Social Media Marketing
- Social Media Optimization
- Web Analytics
- Search Engine Optimization
- Strategic Marketing

Potential Career Advancement: Marketing Director, Head of Digital Team, Digital Marketing Manager, Digital Marketing Director

Educational Qualifications: Bachelor's degree in marketing, communications, any business – related field. MBA in marketing is preferred.

Work Schedule: Hours will depend on the given workload; expect to work during weekends or in some nights to meet deadlines.

Internet Marketing Specialists

The tasks of Internet Marketing Specialists usually involve the following:

- They are in charge of creating online content that are used for advertising a certain brand, product, product features and other services.

- They must be experts in creating content that will be ranked highly by Google and various search engines as it will help audiences to be drawn to their brand online.

- They are the ones monitoring the traffic and performance of various online marketing campaigns. And through monitoring the search engine results and what drives traffic, they can optimize the keywords usage and integrate it to their current marketing campaign.

Estimated Annual Salary: $30,000 to $60,000

Average Annual Salary in the U.S: $40,000

Number of Years and Experience (in the U.S.):

- Around 6% of Internet Marketing Specialists have less than 1 year working experience
- Around 62% of Internet Marketing Specialists have 1 to 4 years working experience
- Around 22% of Internet Marketing Specialists have 5 to 9 years working experience
- Around 9% of Internet Marketing Specialists have 10 to 19 years working experience
- Around 1% of Internet Marketing Specialists have 20 + years working experience

Top Skills Needed:

- Social Media Marketing
- Social Media Optimization
- Online Marketing
- Search Engine Optimization
- Email Marketing

Potential Career Advancement: Marketing Director, Head of Digital Team, Digital Marketing Manager, Digital Marketing Director, Online Marketing Manager

Educational Qualifications: Associate's degree in marketing or business administration is acceptable. Bachelor's degree in marketing, communications, or any business – related field is preferred. Strong background in computer science is a plus.

Work Schedule: Regular business hours

E- Commerce Manager

The tasks of E – Commerce Managers usually involve the following:

- They are usually hired by B2C companies because they are experts when it comes to various ecommerce tools such as Google Analytics, HTML and other e-commerce software.

- They are responsible for how a business or brand will appear online, and they are also tasked in the sales budget, predicting future prospects, updating of pricing and promotions through various e – commerce platforms and they also review the results of a product's performance and sales.

Estimated Annual Salary: $35,000 to $93,000

Average Annual Salary in the U.S: $53,000

Number of Years and Experience (in the U.S.):

- Around 1% of E – Commerce Managers have less than 1 year working experience
- Around 46% of E – Commerce Managers have 1 to 4 years working experience
- Around 29% of E – Commerce Managers have 5 to 9 years working experience

- Around 21% of E – Commerce Managers have 10 to 19 years working experience
- Around 2% of E – Commerce Managers have 20 + years working experience

Top Skills Needed:

- E – Commerce
- Customer Service
- Online Marketing
- Content Management
- Project Management

Potential Career Advancement: Marketing Director, Head of Digital Team, Digital Marketing Director

Educational Qualifications: Bachelor's degree in marketing, or any business – related field is required.

Work Schedule: Regular business hours

Search Engine Optimization (SEO) Manager

The tasks of SEO Managers usually involve the following:

- The primary duty of SEO managers is to improve the search ranking of a particular product, service, brand or company in various search engines or web pages.

- They are in charge of listing a company in various online directories so that whenever customers are searching for a particular product/ service, the brand will be one of the first to appear in web searches.

- They are in charge of creating landing pages, keyword optimization, and web analytics to make sure that the leads online will land on the company's page and turn these searches into paying customers.

Estimated Annual Salary: $40,000 to $88,000

Average Annual Salary in the U.S: $61,000

Number of Years and Experience (in the U.S.):

- 0% of SEO Managers have less than 1 year working experience

- Around 46% of SEO Managers have 1 to 4 years working experience
- Around 43% of SEO Managers have 5 to 9 years working experience
- Around 11% of SEO Managers have 10 to 19 years working experience
- 0% of SEO Managers have 20 + years working experience

Top Skills Needed:

- Search Engine Optimization
- Web Content Management
- Web Analytics
- Search Engine Marketing
- Social Media Marketing

Potential Career Advancement: Digital Marketing Director, Social Media Director

Educational Qualifications: Bachelor's degree in marketing, or any business – related field is required.

Work Schedule: Regular business hours; some positions is offered as teleworking/ freelance

Search Engine Marketing (SEM) Manager

The tasks of SEM Managers usually involve the following:

- SEM Manager usually supervises a team of marketers who are tasked with leveraging search engine promotions in order to increate website traffic, conversions, and sales.

- They must be experts in both the creative, and marketing aspects in order to maximize the advertising budget given by the company and make sure that there will be a return of investments.
- They must also know how to conquer the 3 giant search engine websites namely; Google, Yahoo, and Bing.

Estimated Annual Salary: $41,000 to $91,000

Average Annual Salary in the U.S: $64,000

Number of Years and Experience (in the U.S.):

- Around 1% of SEM Managers have less than 1 year working experience
- Around 56% of SEM Managers have 1 to 4 years working experience
- Around 36% of SEM Managers have 5 to 9 years working experience
- Around 8% of SEM Managers have 10 to 19 years working experience
- 0% of SEM Managers have 20 + years working experience

Top Skills Needed:

- Search Engine Optimization
- Google AdWords
- Web Analytics
- Search Engine Marketing
- Internet Marketing

Potential Career Advancement: Digital Marketing Director, Social Media Director

Educational Qualifications: Bachelor's degree in marketing, computer science, statistics, or any business – related field is required.

Work Schedule: Regular business hours; some positions is offered as teleworking/ freelance.

Paid Search Manager

The tasks of Paid Search Managers usually involve the following:

- Their primary duty is to develop and execute the paid search strategies of a business.

- They should also know how to take advantage of the trends and technological changes online and must know how to use metrics that will evaluate successful paid searches.

- They are also in charge of updating tools and keywords searches and must know how to write reports to improve search engine marketing strategies and conversion.

Estimated Annual Salary: $41,000 to $88,000

Average Annual Salary in the U.S: $61,000

Number of Years and Experience (in the U.S.):

- 0% of Paid Search Managers have less than 1 year working experience
- Around 62% of Paid Search Managers have 1 to 4 years working experience
- Around 29% of Paid Search Managers have 5 to 9 years working experience
- Around 7% of Paid Search Managers have 10 to 19 years working experience
- Around 3% of Paid Search Managers have 20 + years working experience

Top Skills Needed:

- Google AdWords
- Google Analytics
- Search Engine Marketing
- Microsoft Excel

Potential Career Advancement: Digital Marketing Director, SEO Manager, SEM Manager

Educational Qualifications: Bachelor's degree in marketing, computer science, statistics, or any business – related field is preferred.

Work Schedule: Regular business hours; some positions is offered as teleworking/ freelance

Pay – Per – Click (PPC) Manager

The tasks of Pay – Per – Click Managers usually involve the following:

- The primary duties of PPC Mangers include attracting traffic from search engine websites like Google, Yahoo, or Bing, and they must also know search engine optimization duties.

- They usually work with the marketing and design teams to create ads that will improve the click – through rates and be redirected to the company's website. They will be successful if the amount of clicks generated by marketing campaigns met the quota or goals of the company through their strategies.

- They are experts in web analytics and are also in charge of doing consumer – testings and online surveys.

Estimated Annual Salary: $35,000 to $66,000

Average Annual Salary in the U.S: $48,000

Number of Years and Experience (in the U.S.):

- Around 4% of PPC Managers have less than 1 year working experience
- Around 71% of PPC Managers have 1 to 4 years working experience
- Around 19% of PPC Managers have 5 to 9 years working experience
- Around 5% of PPC Managers have 10 to 19 years working experience
- Around 1% of PPC Managers have 20 + years working experience

Top Skills Needed:

- Google AdWords
- Google Analytics
- Search Engine Marketing
- Search Engine Optimization

Potential Career Advancement: Digital Marketing Director, SEO Manager, SEM Manager

Educational Qualifications: Bachelor's degree in marketing, computer science, or any business – related field is required. Experience in Google Adwords is preferred.

Work Schedule: Regular business hours; some positions is offered as teleworking/ freelance.

Chapter Eight: Marketing Communications - Related Positions

    This chapter will focus on the most common positions that are related to marketing communications. Marketing communications is a very important branch of marketing because it helps in promoting the overall message and image of a company and also the brands/ products it carries. They are also mostly in charge of making sure that the product, advertisements, and promotions whether online or offline is accurate and in line with the company's vision and mission. They are also in charge of handling conflict, negative press releases and helps in damage control to protect the company's credibility and reputation.

Communications Director

The tasks of Communications Directors usually involve the following:

- They are in charge of managing the information and message that's being delivered to the target market and to the public.
- They act as the company's spokesperson and they are the ones in charge of holding press conferences, writing press releases, and also responding to questions or interview requests from various journalists and media outlets.

- They also attend programs or events on behalf of the company since they are the representative.

- They are experts when it comes to handling negative circumstances or press, and knows how to do damage control to ensure that the company's image is intact.

Estimated Annual Salary: $38,000 to $116,000

Average Annual Salary in the U.S: $63,000

Number of Years and Experience (in the U.S.):

- Around 1% of Communication Directors have less than 1 year working experience

- Around 22% of Communication Directors have 1 to 4 years working experience
- Around 27% of Communication Directors have 5 to 9 years working experience
- Around 34% of Communication Directors have 10 to 19 years working experience
- Around 16% of Communication Directors have 20 + years working experience

Top Skills Needed:

- Marketing Communications
- Strategic Marketing
- Media/ Public Relations
- Social Media Marketing
- Corporate Communications

Potential Career Advancement: Executive Director or Director of Development for Non – Profit Organizations, Corporate Communications Director, Marketing Communications Director

Educational Qualifications: Bachelor's degree in marketing, communications, or any business – related field is required.

Work Schedule: Regular business hours; may have additional working hours for event management or press release launches.

Communications Manager

The tasks of Communications Managers usually involve the following:

- They help facilitate and mold the internal and external message or image of the company.

- They build connections and relationships to various organizations, other companies, and clientele.

- They usually work with the creative team and marketing team to promote a positive image for the company.

Estimated Annual Salary: $38,000 to $92,000

Average Annual Salary in the U.S: $59,000

Number of Years and Experience (in the U.S.):

- Around 1% of Communication Managers have less than 1 year working experience
- Around 31% of Communication Managers have 1 to 4 years working experience
- Around 35% of Communication Managers have 5 to 9 years working experience
- Around 24% of Communication Managers have 10 to 19 years working experience
- Around 9% of Communication Managers have 20 + years working experience

Top Skills Needed:

- Marketing Communications
- Strategic Marketing
- Media/ Public Relations
- Social Media Marketing
- Corporate Communications
- Project Management

Potential Career Advancement: Marketing Communications Manager, Communication Director, Marketing Director, Senior Manager of Corp. Communications

Educational Qualifications: Bachelor's degree in marketing, communications, journalism or any business – related field is required.

Work Schedule: Regular business hours

Communications Coordinator

The tasks of Communications Coordinators usually involve the following:

- They are in charge of handling tasks in terms of various marketing communications needs inside or outside the company.

- They are also responsible for maintaining the company's reputation not just to the public but also to the employees within the organization.

- They help develop and implement creative marketing projects such as events, and publications.

Estimated Annual Salary: $31,000 to $56,000

Average Annual Salary in the U.S: $39,000

Number of Years and Experience (in the U.S.):

- Around 5% of Communication Coordinators have less than 1 year working experience
- Around 62% of Communication Coordinators have 1 to 4 years working experience
- Around 19% of Communication Coordinators have 5 to 9 years working experience
- Around 10% of Communication Coordinators have 10 to 19 years working experience
- Around 4% of Communication Coordinators have 20 + years working experience

Top Skills Needed:

- Marketing Communications
- Strategic Marketing
- Media/ Public Relations
- Social Media Marketing
- Web Content Management
- Proficiency in MS Office

Potential Career Advancement: Marketing Communications Manager, Communication Director, Marketing Manager, Communications Specialist

Educational Qualifications: Bachelor's degree in marketing, communications, PR, or any business – related field is required.

Work Schedule: Regular business hours

Marketing Communications Manager

The tasks of Marketing Communications Managers usually involve the following:

- They are more focused on marketing endeavors that will promote brand awareness.
- Their main duty is to gain and also maintain a good customer base through developing and executing various advertising/ marketing strategies.
- They also train the marketing staff and helps identify potential competitors to ensure that the company is always ahead of the pack.

Estimated Annual Salary: $42,000 to $93,000

Average Annual Salary in the U.S: $64,000

Number of Years and Experience (in the U.S.):

- Around 1% of Marketing Communications Manager have less than 1 year working experience
- Around 23% of Marketing Communications Manager have 1 to 4 years working experience
- Around 35% of Marketing Communications Manager have 5 to 9 years working experience
- Around 28% of Marketing Communications Manager have 10 to 19 years working experience
- Around 12% of Marketing Communications Manager have 20 + years working experience

Top Skills Needed:

- Marketing Communications
- Strategic Marketing
- Media/ Public Relations
- Branding

Potential Career Advancement: Marketing Communications Manager, Marketing Communication Director, Senior Marketing Manager, Senior Manager of Corp. Communications

Educational Qualifications: Bachelor's degree in marketing, communications, or any business – related field is required.

Work Schedule: Regular business hours

Corporate Communications Manager

The tasks of Corporate Communications Managers usually involve the following:

- Their primary duty is to manage the company's public messaging through drafting and approving company statements.
- They also oversee PR initiatives and they are in charge of looking for partners to further the company's vision and mission.
- They are responsible for handling media inquiries, creating press releases, communicating the company's objectives through marketing campaigns and social media efforts.

Estimated Annual Salary: $51,000 to $105,000

Average Annual Salary in the U.S: $78,000

Number of Years and Experience (in the U.S.):

- 0% of Corporate Communications Manager have less than 1 year working experience
- Around 16% of Corporate Communications Manager have 1 to 4 years working experience
- Around 37% of Corporate Communications Manager have 5 to 9 years working experience
- Around 33% of Corporate Communications Manager have 10 to 19 years working experience
- Around 14% of Corporate Communications Manager have 20 + years working experience

Top Skills Needed:

- Corporate Communications
- Media/ Public Relations
- Social Media Marketing
- Marketing Communications
- Technical Writing

Potential Career Advancement: Corp. Communications Director, VP of Public Relations and Corp. Communications

Educational Qualifications: Bachelor's degree in marketing, communications, PR, or any business – related field is required.

Work Schedule: Regular business hours

Public Relations (PR) Manager

The tasks of Public Relations Managers usually involve the following:

- They are in charge of maintain and improving the company's public image through developing and implementing PR campaigns that will boost brand and company awareness.

- They're also in charge of ensuring that other departments deliver accurate information, and they it's their job to evaluate the success of PR campaigns.

- They can also represent the company to various media outlets.

Estimated Annual Salary: $39,000 to $96,000

Average Annual Salary in the U.S: $61,000

Number of Years and Experience (in the U.S.):

- Around 2% of Public Relations Manager have less than 1 year working experience
- Around 26% of Public Relations Manager have 1 to 4 years working experience
- Around 40% of Public Relations Manager have 5 to 9 years working experience
- Around 25% of Public Relations Manager have 10 to 19 years working experience
- Around 7% of Public Relations Manager have 20 + years working experience

Top Skills Needed:

- Corporate Communications
- Media/ Public Relations
- Social Media Marketing
- Marketing Communications
- MS Office

Potential Career Advancement: Marketing Director, PR
Director, Communications Director, Corp. Communications
Director

Educational Qualifications: Bachelor's degree in marketing,
communications, PR, or any business – related field is
required.

Work Schedule: Regular business hours with minor travel
requirements especially during events, promotions, or
training.

Media Managers

The tasks of Media Managers usually involve the
following:

- Their job is to manage the interactions of the
  company with the media, and they are also in
  charge of improving the effectiveness of press
  strategies and public campaigns.

- They ensure that the company's image is
  consistent and well – coordinated especially in
  cases of crisis or negative news releases.

- They should know how to analyze and evaluate the results of all media – related efforts.

Estimated Annual Salary: $37,000 to $87,000

Average Annual Salary in the U.S: $55,000

Number of Years and Experience (in the U.S.):

- Around 1% of Media Managers have less than 1 year working experience
- Around 46% of Media Managers have 1 to 4 years working experience
- Around 29% of Media Managers have 5 to 9 years working experience
- Around 19% of Media Managers have 10 to 19 years working experience
- Around 6% of Media Managers have 20 + years working experience

Top Skills Needed:

- Media Management
- Advertising
- Strategic Planning
- Marketing Communications

Potential Career Advancement: Media Director

Educational Qualifications: Bachelor's degree in marketing, communications, PR, or any business – related field is required. Master's degree in business administration or communications is preferred.

Travel Requirement: Minor travel may be required

Work Schedule: Regular business hours

Event Managers

The tasks of Event Managers usually involve the following:

- They are in charge of creating and scheduling events such as company conferences, promotions, and even company parties.

- They are in charge of working with clients in order to plan the event that's based on clients' preferences, budget and overall needs.

- Event managers must have exceptional negotiation skills because they'll also be dealing with suppliers and contractors.

Estimated Annual Salary: $33,000 to $70,000

Average Annual Salary in the U.S: $48,000

Number of Years and Experience (in the U.S.):

- Around 2% of Event Managers have less than 1 year working experience
- Around 39% of Event Managers have 1 to 4 years working experience
- Around 33% of Event Managers have 5 to 9 years working experience
- Around 22% of Event Managers have 10 to 19 years working experience
- Around 5% of Event Managers have 20 + years working experience

Top Skills Needed:

- Project Management
- Event Management
- Contract Negotiation
- Event Planning
- Budget Management

Potential Career Advancement: Marketing Manager, Director of Events, Special Events Manager, Senior Event Manager, Catering Sales Manager

Educational Qualifications: Bachelor's degree in marketing, communications, or any business – related field is required.

Travel Requirement: Minor travel may be required especially during events and product promotions

Work Schedule: Regular business hours

Promotions Managers

The tasks of Promotions Managers usually involve the following:

- Promotions Managers are in charge of overseeing promotion programs that aims to raise the point – of – sale transactions in order to encourage more customers to buy certain products. They do it through coming up with advertising deals, promos or other bonuses to entice consumers.

- They're also in charge of implementing promotions strategies and ensures that the in –

store graphics are consistent with the company's/ product's message.

- They also make sure that campaigns are within the company's promotions/ marketing budget.

Estimated Annual Salary: $28,000 to $85,000

Average Annual Salary in the U.S: $46,000

Number of Years and Experience (in the U.S.):

- Around 2% of Promotions Managers have less than 1 year working experience
- Around 39% of Promotions Managers have 1 to 4 years working experience
- Around 33% of Promotions Managers have 5 to 9 years working experience
- Around 21% of Promotions Managers have 10 to 19 years working experience
- Around 6% of Promotions Managers have 20 + years working experience

Top Skills Needed:

- Promotions
- Social Media Marketing
- People Management
- Event Planning
- Marketing Management

Potential Career Advancement: Marketing Manager

Educational Qualifications: High school diploma, Associate's degree is acceptable. Bachelor's degree in marketing, communications, or any business – related field is preferred.

Travel Requirement: Minor travel may be required especially during events and product promotions

Work Schedule: Regular business hours

Chapter Nine: Creative Marketing - Related Positions

This chapter focuses on the positions related to advertising or creative side of marketing. They are mostly tasked to create articles, slogans, logos, designs, and layout for a certain brand or product of the company. The creative marketing – related positions that you'll learn in this chapter are usually a mix of both the traditional advertising and digital marketing which means that they can be flexible in terms of handling various advertising projects. Through their write ups, designs, and advertising skills they are able to deliver the message that their company or client wants to convey.

Copywriters

The tasks of Copywriters usually involve the following:

- A copywriter's job is to create write ups that will be used in advertisements, digital promotions, and various marketing campaigns.
- They must be exceptional when it comes to creating a powerful message by using just a handful of words. They create slogans for brands/ companies as well as catchy ads.
- They usually work directly with the client in order for them to meet their needs and also know the concepts that the client wants to incorporate.

Estimated Annual Salary: $31,000 to $68,000

Average Annual Salary in the U.S: $45,000

Number of Years and Experience (in the U.S.):

- Around 6% of Copywriters have less than 1 year working experience
- Around 58% of Copywriters have 1 to 4 years working experience
- Around 22% of Copywriters have 5 to 9 years working experience

- Around 10% of Copywriters have 10 to 19 years working experience
- Around 4% of Copywriters have 20 + years working experience

Top Skills Needed:

- Copywriting/ Editing
- Media/ Public Relations
- Advertising
- MS Office
- Marketing Communications

Potential Career Advancement: Marketing Director, Senior Copywriter, Creative Director, Marketing Communications Manager, Associate Director of Creative Services.

Educational Qualifications: Bachelor's degree in marketing, communications, PR, or any business – related field is required. Some organizations prefer those with IPA Foundation certificate

Travel Requirement: Minor travel may be required

Work Schedule: Regular business hours with longer hours every now and then to meet deadlines.

Media Buyer

The tasks of Media Buyers usually involve the following:

- Their main duty is to buy the media "real estate" – the media real estate usually includes ad space on the internet, radio, TV and other media outlets such as billboards, transportation ads spaces, grocery ad spaces etc.

- They should also be knowledgeable in using analytics because this is how they're going to know what media outlet will be the best suited for their target audience.

- They're in charge of evaluating the consumers' response to an ad or ad space.

Estimated Annual Salary: $33,000 to $60,000

Average Annual Salary in the U.S: $44,000

Number of Years and Experience (in the U.S.):

- Around 4% of Media Buyers have less than 1 year working experience

- Around 59% of Media Buyers have 1 to 4 years working experience
- Around 18% of Media Buyers have 5 to 9 years working experience
- Around 13% of Media Buyers have 10 to 19 years working experience
- Around 6% of Media Buyers have 20 + years working experience

Top Skills Needed:

- Media Management
- Advertising
- Account Management
- Proficiency in MS Excel

Potential Career Advancement: Media Director, Media Supervisor, Media Planner, Social Media Planner

Educational Qualifications: High school diploma, Associate's degree is acceptable. Bachelor's degree in marketing, communications, or any business – related field is preferred.

Travel Requirement: Minor travel may be required

Work Schedule: Regular business hours

Creative Director

The tasks of Creative Directors usually involve the following:

- Creative Directors usually leads a creative team and he/she is in charge of developing and executing creative work in various media fields such as advertising, graphics, music, TV, movies, and other media channels.

- They can either be an in – house creative director or they could be working for an agency and deals directly with clients.

- The job of in – house creative directors usually involve creating various media and marketing tasks for a certain department/ brand within the company that they work for. On the other hand, creative directors working in an agency usually handle creative projects for various types of client needs.

Estimated Annual Salary: $44,000 to $152,000

Average Annual Salary in the U.S: $85,000

Number of Years and Experience (in the U.S.):

- Around 1% of Creative Directors have less than 1 year working experience
- Around 13% of Creative Directors have 1 to 4 years working experience
- Around 20% of Creative Directors have 5 to 9 years working experience
- Around 45% of Creative Directors have 10 to 19 years working experience
- Around 21% of Creative Directors have 20 + years working experience

Top Skills Needed:

- Adobe Photoshop
- Branding
- Adobe Illustrator
- Graphic Design

Potential Career Advancement: Marketing Manager, Marketing Communications Director, Marketing Director, VP of Marketing, Creative Services Director

Educational Qualifications: Bachelor's degree in marketing or communications is required with specialization in advertising, graphic design or any similar field is required.

Work Schedule: Regular business hours

Art Director

The tasks of Art Directors usually involve the following:

- Art Directors usually oversee the creative or artistic works of the design/ graphics team.

- They approve the message, design, and layout of the creative work.

- He/ she should be knowledgeable in using various digital design tools such as Adobe Photoshop so that he/she can better supervise the graphics team.

- They usually work with graphic designers, creative directors, copywriters, photographers, videographers etc. and sets project deadlines to the staff.

Estimated Annual Salary: $40,000 to $94,000

Average Annual Salary in the U.S: $62,000

Number of Years and Experience (in the U.S.):

- Around 1% of Art Directors have less than 1 year working experience
- Around 21% of Art Directors have 1 to 4 years working experience
- Around 28% of Art Directors have 5 to 9 years working experience
- Around 34% of Art Directors have 10 to 19 years working experience
- Around 16% of Art Directors have 20 + years working experience

Top Skills Needed:

- Adobe Photoshop
- Branding
- Adobe Illustrator
- Graphic Design

Potential Career Advancement: Senior Art Director, Creative Director, Associate Director of Creative Services, Creative Services Director, Creative Services Manger

Educational Qualifications: Bachelor's degree in marketing or communications is required with specialization in advertising, graphic design or any similar field is required.

Work Schedule: Regular business hours

Graphic Designer

The tasks of Graphic Designers usually involve the following:

- They are the ones who use various illustration and layout techniques to visually communicate the brand message of a certain product/ service.
- They are in charge of creating logos, product packaging, web designs, brochures, posters, infographics online, and print materials for the company/ product.
- Many graphic designers work with the creative/ advertising/ marketing teams within a company but some are also hired as freelancers.

- Most graphic designers specialize in a few areas like poster making, web design, corporate identity/ logos, or print/ packaging.

Estimated Annual Salary: $30,000 to $60,000

Average Annual Salary in the U.S: $39,000

Number of Years and Experience (in the U.S.):

- Around 3% of Graphic Designers have less than 1 year working experience
- Around 48% of Graphic Designers have 1 to 4 years working experience
- Around 26% of Graphic Designers have 5 to 9 years working experience
- Around 16% of Graphic Designers have 10 to 19 years working experience
- Around 7% of Graphic Designers have 20 + years working experience

Top Skills Needed:

- Graphic Design
- Adobe Photoshop
- Adobe Illustrator
- Branding

Potential Career Advancement: Senior Graphic Designer, Art Director, Creative Director, Web Designer

Educational Qualifications: Bachelor's degree in marketing or communications is required with specialization in advertising, graphic design or any similar field is required.

Work Schedule: Regular business hours

Chapter Ten: Landing Your First Job

This chapter will focus on some of the most important things you need to remember when it comes to starting your career path in marketing. We'll briefly discuss the methods on how you can determine which particular marketing position is right for you by identifying what you want. The position and the company you'll work for should be in line with your personal values, with your interests as well as your skills and experiences. After knowing what you're inclined to do, you'll get some tips on where you can start applying for jobs and also how you can create a clear and concise CV that's full of content. We've also highlighted the

---

timeless tips on how you can nail your job interview and get your dream marketing job! Good luck!

Find Out What You Want!

Knowing exactly what your interests and passions are, is very essential as you start your marketing career journey, this will help you target the potential job you like as well as the company or employer that will best suit you. Here are the factors to consider when looking for a job or career that will best resonate with your passions/ interests:

- **Location:** Where do you want to work? Are there any areas you particularly want to be based in? Financial districts and large cities will remain as the hub for various marketing career opportunities whereas rural areas might have limited marketing jobs available. Decide where you want to start gaining some working experience.

- **Passion and Hobbies:** What areas of marketing, communication, or business are you particularly interested in? What intellectually stimulates you? What are you inclined to do with regards to marketing aspects?

- **Salary and Position:** What is your target position or where do you want to be a couple of years from now? Obviously you have to start somewhere but it's best that you already know where you want to go or at least where you might want to end up in because this will ultimately help you to plan out your career. How much do you want to get paid at the onset? How much is your target annual income?

- **Work Conditions:** Do you prefer working in a high – pressured environment or would you like to be somewhere relatively relaxed? Working in high – pressured environment might be stressful but you'll surely learn A LOT of things and you'll develop various marketing skills that'll help you in the future.

- **Values:** What are your values? Knowing what you value and what your potential employer value (through their vision/ mission) must coincide with the values you personally uphold so that you will feel that you're contributing in something that you're proud of.

- **People/ Colleagues:** What kind of people do you want to work with? Do you prefer those who are tech – savvy/ analytical? More creative? Or perhaps those who are more social? This will help you determine which marketing department you might potentially thrive on because at some point you need to collaborate with people – and you would want to work with people that will bring out the best in you.

Let the Job Hunting Begin!

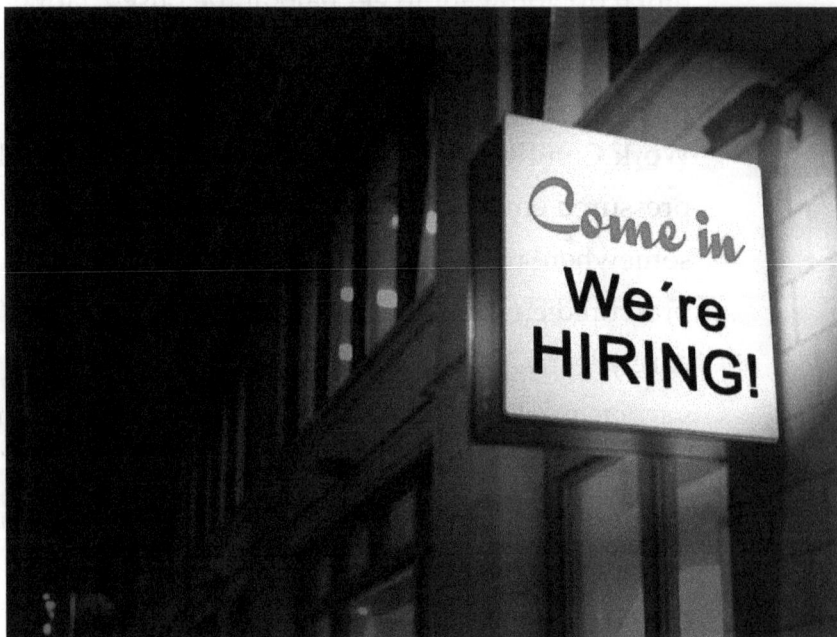

This section will show you the various avenues where you can potentially find your dream marketing job. Check out the following avenues and don't hesitate to submit your application to all of them. The more chances, the better!

Graduation Schemes

Companies usually run graduate schemes in various universities at least once a year so make sure that you read all the information found on the company's website where you want to apply and incorporate all the advice they have for aspirants like you. Attend their events and show them that you are committed.

Direct to Companies

If you want to specifically apply in a company that may not be included in job fairs at your school or community then its best that you directly send them your application. Check out their website and see if there are vacant positions where you can be qualified. If ever no marketing – related position is advertised, consider sending them your CV anyway so that if anything comes up they can reach out to you. It's also best to find a direct point of contact like an HR associate where you can follow up your application.

Recruitment Agencies

If you apply through recruitment agencies, you'll most likely get feedback and tips on how you can nail your job interview. It's their job to get you employed because that's how they'll get paid as a recruitment agent. They will definitely help you demonstrate yourself as a potential candidate and will connect you to the best employers so make sure to put effort into your application before sending it to them.

Job boards

Another great place to find jobs is through checking out various job sites because these are excellent places to find a potential job. Salaries, job responsibilities, education and working requirements are almost always posted.

Networking

Getting a job or a career opportunity is sometimes knowing the right people. As the saying goes, "it's not about what you know; it's about who you know." Sometimes jobs aren't always advertised but if you know someone working inside your prospective company, he/she can personally recommend you to your prospective employer if any positions are available provided of course that you somehow have a great relationship with this person. They could be your friends, relatives, and even acquaintances.

Tips in Writing an Effective Curriculum Vitae

Here are some practical tips that'll help you prepare your resume or Curriculum Vitae (CV) as well as your cover letter.

Tip #1: Simplicity is the best sophistication

- **Keep your CV or resume and your cover letter as simple as possible.** As Steve Jobs said, "Simplicity is the best sophistication," it must be easy to read and doesn't contain fluff words. The standard font size is 12 and the font style could be Arial, Times New Roman or anything similar. Make sure to use section headings so that the details will look organized; it's also best to use bold fonts, bullets, and small – length paragraphs to highlight key points and make it very clear for the reader because usually recruiters/ hiring managers just scan the applications so you need to make sure that it's clear, concise, and has content.

Tip #2: Highlight your experiences

- **Quantify your skills and working experiences.**
What recruiters and hiring managers look for in each position is two things: (1) What you did (2) How well you did it. As an example, if you're applying for a social media manager, you must highlight in your resume any experience related to you handling social media accounts or perhaps your own personal page; you have to tell them how you've grown your followers or what strategies did you apply to reach a certain goal. You have to showcase what you did (e.g. Increased social media followers from 100 to 1,000 in just 3 months through applying digital marketing skills like SEO, videos etc.). You can further explain on how you did it in your cover letter.

Tip #3: Make it perfect!

- **Scrutinize your own work and triple check for any errors.** You must make sure that there's no error in spellings, punctuations and grammar. The formatting and details must also be consistent with your cover letter. Have it edited or hire a proofreader if need be. Sometimes tiny details are the cause of rejected applications so ensure that every single detail is "perfect." If ever your application should be submitted online, then print it and double check it before sending.

Here's a sample CV and cover letter that you can use as a guide:

Sample Curriculum Vitae

MARIANNE KAMPA

2222 University Drive
St. Louis, MO 63130
123-555-5555

1

linkedin.com/in/marianne-kampa
iheartplayingcroquet@gmail.com

6363 Merry Lane
Caperberry, IL 60000
456-555-5555

2 **EDUCATION**
WASHINGTON UNIVERSITY, OLIN BUSINESS SCHOOL, St. Louis, MO   **4** **September 2017-Present**
BSBA **3**
Majors in Finance and Economics and Strategy; Minor in Healthcare Management
- Overall GPA: 3.70/4.00
- Dean's List

EXPERIENCE
CAPITAL ONE, Richmond, VA   June 2019-August 2019
Business Analyst Intern
5 I developed Excel-based analysis models to study effective revenue strategies, together with cross-functional team members, and presented findings to mentor team; I analyzed written and verbal customer feedback on credit product terms and provided recommendations regarding terms to supervisor; finally, I gained an understanding of Capital One's products and the credit industry through independent and group projects, seminars, personal mentoring, and other development opportunities

SKANDALARIS INTERNSHIP PROGRAM—ANNOUNCE MEDIA, St. Louis, MO   June 2018-August 2018
The Skandalaris Internship Program combined a 10-week entrepreneurial internship at St. Louis startup Announce Media with a leadership development program.
Client Development Summer Intern
- Researched customers and set up meetings to get new accounts
- Updated social media sites with new company announcements **6**
- Sat in on informational presentations

ST. LOUIS CHILDREN'S HOSPITAL, St. Louis, MO   Summer 2017
St. Louis Children's Hospital is one of the premier healthcare institutions for children in the United States.
Finance Department Intern
- Filed papers in an organized manner
- Answered patient's questions and took messages for other staff in office

ACTIVITIES **7**

- *VP of Finance*–DSP **8**
- *Member*–Intramural Coed Frisbee Team
- *Volunteer*–Each One Teach One

SKILLS

- Computer Skills: Microsoft Word, PowerPoint, Access, Excel
- **9** Language Skills: Familiar with Spanish
- Interests: Playing croquet, helicopters, jumping rope, reading about current events, and watching news programs **10**

Sample Cover Letter

1234 University Way, Campus Box 567 ①
St. Louis, MO 63130

October 3, 2018

John Spencer ②
Director of College Recruiting
Wells Fargo
One North Jefferson Avenue
St. Louis, MO 63103

Dear Mr. Spencer:

③ I am writing in regard to the Wells Fargo Advisors Analyst position posted in Washington University's CAREERlink system. I am a senior at Washington University's Olin Business School pursuing a major in finance and a minor in accounting. I immediately became interested in this opportunity after speaking with Sarah Harper at Olin Business School's Meet the Firms event. Wells Fargo's continued success in a challenging marketplace initially motivated me to seek out Wells Fargo at the Career Fair. Further, Ms. Harper described the level of interaction and communication within the company among all levels, from senior management to the client, striving toward a common goal of "what's right for the customer," ④ which really emulates the type of team-based environment I thrive in. Lastly, Wells Fargo's commitment and value placed on developing its team members through education, mentoring, and finding the right fit within the organization make me excited to grow my career in such an organization.

I believe that my employment would be highly beneficial to Wells Fargo, as I possess not only the analytical skills required to be a successful analyst but the organizational and project management skills as well. While interning at Holbrook & Company last summer, I collaborated with senior managers throughout the entire mergers and acquisition process for a major $50 million financial services deal. I created valuation models for various aspects of the deal, as well as compiled and organized pitch books. The experience provided exposure to the process and enhanced my analytical skills and ability to effectively communicate financial information to clients. While studying abroad in London last spring, I had an internship at the trading desk of Citigroup, which allowed me to gain in-depth knowledge of the energy sector in the UK through researching historical financial data and effective communication with company executives, analysts, and investment representatives. This understanding allowed me to better ⑤ advise traders on profitable investment opportunities, resulting in a 7 percent increase in returns in that sector. I am excited to apply these skills, as well as my work ethic, to Wells Fargo.

Thank you for your time and consideration. I look forward to further discussing with you my enthusiasm for Wells Fargo and how I can be an asset to the firm. Please feel free to contact me at 314-555-4444 or ⑥ janson@wustl.edu if you have any further questions. I also look forward to seeing you on campus on October 19, 2018.

Sincerely,

Jerome Janson

Attachment: Résumé

Nailing Your Job Interview

Here are the most important tips that any applicant should do once they've been scheduled for a job interview. This also applies to any type of positions or jobs you will undertake in the future.

Tip #1: Consider the Logistics

- Make sure to get the basics taken care of such as the time/ schedule of your interview, the location (what floor, what building, what department, what office), the contact person, the clothes you'll wear, the routes/

transportation you'll take on the day, the documents you'll need to bring etc. You need to prepare for this at least a few days before your scheduled interview to avoid any unforeseen circumstances as much as possible and for you to focus on the most important thing – your job interview. You need to be relaxed on the day of the interview by ensuring that these tiny logistics are taken care off. Make sure to arrive early so that you'll have ample time to prepare yourself.

Tip #2: Do your own due diligence

- Make sure that you do your "homework" through research or due diligence. You need to know key things about the company, the products/ services they offer, latest updates in the company and the industry, the important people within the company etc. The more you know about the company that you're applying to, the higher chances of success for getting the job.

Tip #3: Know your CV and anticipate questions

- In addition to questions related about the company, you'll most likely be asked regarding the details written in your CV/ resume so make sure that you know it by heart or at least you know how to justify the skills/ experiences you have written. It's also best that you anticipate the questions a hiring manager might have which will be most likely related to marketing – their goal is to know if you are really capable of doing the job and your work ethic in general. They will most likely asked you questions that's related to your values, your strengths/ weaknesses, how you work with others, how you respond to certain circumstances like if any problems come up, and how you can specifically contribute to the company's success. You will definitely not guess every question and may not nail everything but what's important is that you've come prepared and you're confident.

Tip #4: Be mentally prepared

- Don't stress out too much! If you're too nervous you'll get mentally blocked by the time questions are thrown at you; you wouldn't want to stammer and struggle during your interview because this will decrease your confidence. Make sure that you're relaxed, and try to control your nerves. Sleep early the night before and just think positive.

Tip #5: First Impression Lasts

- It's one of the oldest cliché but it's the truth. The way you dress, the way you shake hands, and the way you carry and present yourself will set the mood for the whole interview so just relax, smile, be confident, and just believe that you can nail it. If you do that, the interviewer will surely feel relaxed as well and he/she will be impressed with your confidence in no time. Show them that you're the perfect catch! Now go and nail it! You're dream job awaits!

Chapter Ten: Landing Your First Job

Photo Credits

Page 13 Photo by user geralt via Pixabay.com,

https://pixabay.com/en/interaction-social-media-abstract-1233873/

Page 17 Photo by user ar130405 via Pixabay.com,

https://pixabay.com/en/business-search-seo-engine-2082639/

Page 19 Photo by user igorovsyannykov via Pixabay.com,

https://pixabay.com/en/stock-shopping-city-background-3170020/

Page 24 Photo by user FirmBee via Pixabay.com,

https://pixabay.com/en/ux-design-webdesign-app-mobile-787980/

Page 26 Photo by user rawpixel via Pixabay.com,

https://pixabay.com/en/analyzing-people-brainstorming-3441040/

Page 27 Photo by user rawpixel via Pixabay.com,

https://pixabay.com/en/activity-adult-book-business-2286443/

Page 40 Photo by user rawpixel via Pixabay.com,

https://pixabay.com/en/analyzing-audience-board-3565815/

Page 46 Photo by user Mediamodifier via Pixabay.com,

https://pixabay.com/en/business-architecture-bar-graph-3033199/

Page 52 Photo by user rawpixel via Pixabay.com,

https://pixabay.com/en/agreement-brainstorming-business-3408113/

Page 58 Photo by user JeShootScom via Pixabay.com,

https://pixabay.com/en/laptop-woman-education-study-young-3087585/

Page 74 Photo by user lbragg1 via Pixabay.com,

https://pixabay.com/en/graduation-graduation-cap-2394130/

Page 97 Photo by user StockSnap via Pixabay.com,

https://pixabay.com/en/laptop-computer-browser-research-2561221/

Page 119 Photo by user Falkenpost via Pixabay.com,

https://pixabay.com/en/signs-road-signs-usa-america-1638668/

Page 149 Photo by user Muneebfarman via Pixabay.com,

https://pixabay.com/en/online-marketing-internet-marketing-1246457/

Page 170 Photo by user Free – Photos via Pixabay.com,

https://pixabay.com/en/workplace-team-business-meeting-1245776/

Page 183 Photo by user Andres_Photos via Pixabay.com,

https://pixabay.com/en/light-lights-night-darkness-notion-1771722/

Page 186 Photo by user rawpixel via Pixabay.com,

https://pixabay.com/en/business-adult-people-office-3365365/

Page 193 Photo by user geralt via Pixabay.com,

https://pixabay.com/en/building-neon-sign-communication-804526/

Page 197 Photo by user rawpixel via Pixabay.com,

https://pixabay.com/en/man-woman-group-teamwork-3365368/

References

"Marketing Careers Guide" – Trackmaven.com
https://trackmaven.com/blog/marketing-careers-guide/

"Digital Marketing and E – Commerce Careers Guide for Students and Graduates" – MBS.edu.gr
http://www.mbs.edu.gr/site_files/digital-marketing-and-e-commerce-careers-guide-for-students-and-graduates.pdf

"The New Grads Guide to Marketing Careers" – Mediabistro.com
file:///C:/Users/jhjn/Downloads/Mediabistro-New-Grads-Guide-Marketing-Careers.pdf

"Personal and Career Development" – Wake Forest University
http://career.opcd.wfu.edu/explore-careers/marketing-and-sales/

"Marketing Degrees and Careers – at – a – Glance" – LearnHowtoBecome.org
https://www.learnhowtobecome.org/finance-business-careers/marketing/

"Job Hunting Decisions and Tips" – TargetJobs.co.uk
https://targetjobs.co.uk/career-sectors/marketing-advertising-and-pr/advice

"Career Opportunities in Marketing" – OSU.edu
http://glenn.osu.edu/career/guides-resources/career-guides/Career%20Opportunities%20in%20Marketing%20(2).pdf

"The Marketing Skills Handbook" – LinkedIn & HubSpot
http://karafarini.atu.ac.ir/uploads/marketing_skills_handbook_eng_us.pdf

"Career Tracks: A Guide for Selecting Careers in Marketing" – Lehigh.edu
https://cbe.lehigh.edu/sites/cbe.lehigh.edu/files/documents/marketingcareertrack2015-revised925.pdf

"Careers in Advertising, Marketing and Public Relations" – University of Chicago
https://careeradvancement.uchicago.edu/sites/default/files/docs/ucis/ucib/careersinadvertising-marketing-publicrelations.pdf

---

"Marketing – Communications Career Guide: How to Break Into Marcom" – IconicDisplays.com
https://www.iconicdisplays.com/wp/marketing-communications-career-guide/

"Adweek's 2017 Graduate's Guide to Marketing and Media" – AdWeek.com

https://www.adweek.com/brand-marketing/adweeks-2017-graduates-guide-to-marketing-and-media/

www.ingramcontent.com/pod-product-compliance
Lightning Source LLC
Chambersburg PA
CBHW060020210326
41520CB00009B/944